Winning the White House In 2016

A Conservative Platform That Will Win the Popular Vote

Tom. E. Porter

Contents

Comments from the Author

The politics of division must forever be ended. It does not matter if you are a Democrat, a Republican, an Independent or a Libertarian. We are all U.S. Citizens. We all strive to improve our lives, to improve the lives of our children and to obtain some level of financial security. We are at our best when we work together to build a better future for our children and at our worst when our leaders intentionally divide us. We are at our best when we embrace and enhance personal freedom and liberty for all U.S. Citizens and at our worst when we force our citizens to comply with rules that constrain freedom. We are at our best when we provide an economy that builds up the middle class and we are at our worst when we are destroying it. We are at our best when we provide the poor with a pathway out of poverty and we are at our worst when all we offer are social service programs and high unemployment. We can do so much better, when we are together.

Unfortunately, we have a leader who is dividing us, berating our historical accomplishments, belittling our values, questioning our character, and filling us with self-doubt and self-loathing. He is leading us into darkness and out of the light. He is making the rich richer and the poor poorer; all the while he is claiming to be our champion. He is not!

This work is focused on us, the U.S. Citizen. I believe there is a war upon us and we are losing. This work presents to you, the most critical voter issues, and offers solutions that will unite us as a people and will support the areas that are most important to us.

There is a military phrase that has become part of our lexicon. It simply says, "I've got your 6." It refers to the face of a clock, with the 12 o'clock position being your face and the 6 o'clock position your back. The proposals in this work, if implemented, will watch the U.S. Citizen's "6".

We can have a much better economy offering high quality jobs, more opportunity, more liberty and more

i

freedom. We can have a government that does not lie to us nor sell us out to the highest campaign contributor. We should expect it and we most certainly deserve it.

As a starting point, you should know that we are in a very, very deep hole. If our country was a business, we would be insolvent. We owe more in current debt and unfunded liabilities than the value of our entire country. Further, you should be aware that leading business analysts are estimating that the number of U. S. Citizens in the middle class is expected to be cut in half in the next 10 years. Conversely, the number of people in the middle class in Asia is expected to triple. This book is your wake up call. This is a clarion call to all U.S. Citizens that you need to read this book, make up your mind and cast your vote for your own welfare, not for the welfare of the special interests. This is your country and your government!

This plan is bold and it leverages our country's advantages to work best for us, not for the special interests or the global citizens or the banks or Wall Street or the environmentalists or the trial attorneys. It entails a lot of heavy lifting, something that our current politicians are not willing or able to perform. In addition, this plan does not sacrifice anyone's principals or values. It is a plan that encompasses the best interests of the majority of our U.S. Citizens. We are, for a change, to be considered first, last and always.

Disclaimer

The thoughts, ideas and opinions expressed in this book are my own and do not represent the thoughts of any other individual or political party. They are offered as advice and advice only. The facts referenced are directionally correct; they do not represent any finite, exact amount. It is the overall size and direction of these facts that raises my concerns and forms the basis for my advice. Individual company data was obtained from the company's individual web sites.

CHAPTER 1
We are Headed in the Wrong Direction

I have been fortunate enough to have traveled to many different countries around the globe and the one comment I always heard from the locals was that "America works". In so many third world countries nothing works. That is why their citizens are trying so hard to come to the USA. They know firsthand what it is like to live with a corrupt government. Their tax money is stolen by corrupt politicians and by the companies they hire for government projects. In their countries, the politicians take care of the wealthy families, leaving the remainder to fend for themselves.

Russia is a good example. Look at the projects associated with the recent Winter Olympics. Hotel rooms had toilets that did not work; doors that did not lock and showers that spat water that was not safe to drink. The same is true for most of the Central and South American countries.

In contrast, most things in the USA work. Generation after generation improved this country and prided themselves on the fact that they left our country in better shape than when they received it. We strived to give our children a better life. We expected them to build upon our lives and lead more successful lives than ours. Now it seems that the upward direction of this country has been reversed. The USA no longer works and what is worse; many U.S. Citizens no longer work! Our government implements programs which reward wealthy families while it offers minimal safety net programs to one third of our citizens. All the while, our once thriving middle class is slipping into poverty and no one is offering a solution. Our government spends lavishly on failed companies and protects the profits of wrong doers. Sounds a lot like a third world country! Together we can change our present course.

In The Beginning

Before we were a country, we were a group of independent colonies ruled by an English Monarch and his Parliament. The colonies had no representation in his majesty's government; as they were not allowed a seat in Parliament. Out of sight was out of mind; so, George III and Parliament felt no compunction about writing punitive laws and regulations as well as levying capricious and burdensome taxes. If the colonists expressed their displeasure, they were told to comply. If they would not comply, they were compelled to comply. One way or the other, his majesty's government was determined to quiet and control an increasingly belligerent group of subjects. It is not difficult to understand why this form of governing fermented unrest and an eventual revolt.

What resulted from this revolt was the creation of the most unique form of government on this Earth. The key factor that made this transition possible was a relatively small group of well educated and determined men whom, together with their followers, revolted against the world's most powerful country. These few men risked everything for the sake of an idea, that men could exercise self-rule and that freedom and liberty were the right of every man.

They risked their very lives, the lives of their family members as well as their fortunes in order to create this

3

country. Not a country where they would replace one oppressive government with another; rather they built for us a country where the citizens themselves are the government. What a concept! This new form of government provided and ensured liberties and freedoms that no other government had ever given to its citizens. But we soon learned that this form of government placed great demands upon its citizens, as many other nations were keen to enslave such a free people. But the challenges to our country were met time and time again by free men and women who cherished our country; men and women who paid with their blood and their treasure in order to maintain this form of government for future generations.

Today we are experiencing a new challenge to our system of government. Today, our major challenges are not coming to us from an outside force; rather, they are coming from within. Identifying these threats and offering solutions is what this book is about.

Now it's our watch. What kind of country are we going to pass on to the next generation? Will they enjoy all the freedoms and liberties that were granted to us? Maintaining freedom and liberty is our responsibility.

CHAPTER 2

We Were Once A Country Of Achievers
Now We Are A Country Of Compliers

Our founding fathers and the many men and women who followed, dedicated their lives in service to this country because they believed in the founding ideals and principles upon which this country was built. They knew that to serve meant their lives were no longer about themselves but rather about our citizens. A fact that is sorely missing with today's crop of politicians.

Today, we have the complete opposite in a President. Obama is all about Obama and he has a White House full of people who are also all about Obama. Here is a man who selectively enforces only those laws with which he agrees, and ignores those with which he does not agree. Not stopping there, he is rewriting laws according to his party's political needs. Clearly this is an abuse of Presidential power. And to top it off, this man openly and callously lies to us. He lavishly spends our tax money on frivolous and self aggrandizing actions like spending $100,000 to fly his dog to join the family on vacation. This is a man who feels our pain? There is no pain in his life; only in ours.

Our national press is cut from the same cloth. Life is all about them and the U.S. Citizen need only be spoon fed their

5

unique version of the day's news; the sum total of which is to make the Democrats look good. They are no longer the lauded Fifth Estate that reveled in bedeviling our politicians and keeping them honest. They are no longer the men and women who honed their journalistic skills by calling foul when any politician did not act in the best interests of the U.S. Citizens. Today, they are the Democrat's propaganda machine; doing their best to destroy the values, ideals and principles upon which this country was built. Their own actions have earned them the name "DemoPress". It is most unfortunate, but for many of us, they are no longer relevant.

As for the entire Democrat Party, they have also earned the name "DemoParty". They are the self-serving demolishers of freedom and liberty. **In truth, the DemoParty is clearly defined by three words: "You Will Comply"**. This is their chosen formula for success and they are using it on all of us.

Allow me to give you a few examples of "You Will Comply" (YWC's). ObamaCare is packed with all kinds of YWC's. For starters, they force you to buy a health insurance policy of their choosing or you will be financially punished. The fact that the DemoParty is compelling you to do things that are not in your best financial interest does not matter to them or to the DemoPress. You can no longer buy the cheaper insurance policy that is better suited to your individual needs and wants. The individual no longer matters, only the groups supporting the DemoParty matter. You and I are forced to comply! You will only be able to see a doctor of their

6

choosing or you will be financially punished. You will only be allowed to go to the hospitals of their choosing or you will be financially punished. You will only buy the healthcare policies that they choose on the government website or you cannot qualify for a subsidy. If you earn too much money you will be punished by higher premiums and higher deductibles and no subsidy. If you earn too little money, you are eligible for a subsidy, but do not earn more than you claimed at the beginning of the year or you will be billed for some or all of the subsidies you received. Confused? Me too! Bottom line, the DemoParty pays you to earn less and use more subsidies.

If you are a Health Care Company you are constantly told to comply or be severely punished...

If you are a coal company or own stock in a coal company you are a polluter... YWC.

If you are an oil company or own stock in an oil company... YWC.

If you are a financial institution... YWC with our new stifling rules.

Their trick is to place themselves between you and everything and everybody in your life. By positioning themselves in this manner, they can control every aspect of your life. It is simple and it works.

They are between you and your...

- Electric Company... The DemoParty EPA will dramatically raise the price of electricity.
- Gas for your car... driving is polluting, buy a new

7

smaller and less safe automobile.

- Clothes Dryer... they no longer dry your clothes... the ones that worked used too much electricity... YWC
- Dishwasher... they no longer dry your dishes... you get it... YWC
- Toilet... they wasted water so they cut the tank capacity in half and now they don't flush as well but... YWC
- Light Bulb... even the Republicans got in on this one; goodbye to the incandescent bulb... YWC
- Automobile... all new cars have a Black Box which will record all events before an accident and will be used against you by every trial lawyer...trial lawyers are the DemoParty's favorite source of money... YWC
There is yet another one for your automobile...they now want to put a real time tracking device in your vehicle that will communicate your vehicle's speed, location and the direction, all in real time and could eventually allow them to control your car remotely. It just keeps getting better and better!
- Freedom of Selection... that is a problem to be controlled... YWC
- Doctor/Hospital/Prescriptions... Cancer patients are losing covered access to their life saving drugs thanks to ObamaCare... YWC even if it kills you!
- Phone Conversations with friends and family... the DemoParty's favorite privacy invading tool is the NSA...

8

- Email with your friends and family... more NSA
- Text... keeping them on file forever to be used against you at some future date
- Thermostat... They are now pushing for the implementation of Smart Thermostats...a device that reports immediately your electricity usage by the minute, hour, day and month. The DemoParty is watching you... YWC
- Your Religion... you will provide birth control and the morning after pill, the DemoParty stands between you and your religion... YWC!
- NFL Team... the DemoParty has come between you and your mascot's name... YWC
- Cellphone... the NSA was not doing enough privacy invading so the U.S. Marshals joined the party and they are employing a new device that tricks your cellphone into thinking that it is hooking up to a normal cellphone tower, but in reality it is connected to their device. They are scooping up everyone's cellphone registration data in the USA under a program called Stingray. So they are now coming between you and your cellphone providers.
- And there is more...

The DemoPress thought they were immune to the DemoParty's YWC's, but they found out what it means to be made to comply. The FCC pushed a White House proposal

9

to place a government monitor in all press rooms. This monitor's purpose was to make sure that the press presents the news with a more favorable slant toward the DemoParty.

This proposed monitor was to question every reporter and editor about how they choose what stories to run. What a laugh! The DemoPress was not doing a good enough job on the propaganda front for the DemoParty. Well the DemoPress has never defended the Second Amendment when it comes under fire from the left; and they did not care when our religious freedoms were under fire by ObamaCare, so I wonder if a direct attack on the freedom of the press will finally get the press on the side of freedom and liberty. The press howled and the FCC put a temporary hold on this program. I think it was a warning shot to shake up the press and let them know that they had better comply with the DemoParty White House.

Mark my words, I truly believe that the DemoParty is far from finished with their attempts to control the press. This has only been a temporary setback. It will not be long before they are going after the internet sites that post any criticism about the DemoParty or the Demo White House. They will come in a side door or a back door and call it something else entirely, maybe even a fairness doctrine or internet security or net neutrality, but their aim will be to control freedom of speech. It will happen most likely in the months leading up to the 2016 election. Maybe I am wrong, but I do not think so!

The Democrats also inserted themselves between the Senate Republicans and long standing, historic Senate Rules.

10

They changed the filibuster rules because they could not get their way. The Senate Republicans were now irrelevant, as the DemoParty packed the courts with their freedom-demolishing candidates. The Republicans never responded to this Democrat Strategy. Now, we must live with the DemoParty's judicial picks for the next 20 years. In addition, the DemoParty President is literally rewriting laws and writing new laws and still the Republicans do not know what to do. The Republicans are not bold when boldness is required. The DemoParty is very bold and their boldness needs to be met with boldness. I propose an answer in Chapter 18.

If you are an ordinary citizen and you dare speak up, the DemoParty will do everything in their power to destroy you and silence you. They will have every applicable enforcement agency go through your life with a fine tooth comb. And they can do it with no fear of an investigation because they own the Department of Justice.

Let's not forget the DemoParty's version of the NSA. They have labeled all of us as potential terrorists. Therefore, we need to be spied upon. They want to be sure that we are following all of their YWC's. Of course, these fine upstanding folks would never use this information in any inappropriate way; would they? They tell us that they are protecting us from harm, so they must spy on all of us. If they only spied on the communities that actually sponsored and supported terrorism, then they would not need to spy on all of us. So say goodbye to liberty and freedom and any right to privacy. They spy on the president of IBM and the president of Apple and every little old lady in Texas and every young woman in Pennsylvania; they spy on their constituents and their political enemies. They spy on us all. But, they had better not spy on Senator Dianne Feinstein because she is special. But it seems that the Executive Branch was spying on her. They knew she was on the Senate Rules Committee and the Select Committee on Intelligence. They were after information regarding the DemoParty's report on the CIA's interrogation program. She was understandably upset. On the other hand, she was fine with all of us being spied upon. I suppose personal privacy only applies to her and her fellow politicians.

There is one other area where the NSA could have played a more active role in protecting our U.S. Citizens; but instead they chose to exploit it to our disadvantage. The issue was the Heartbleed Bug that was present in open source software used by many websites. The NSA knew about it for 2 years and did not warn the U.S. Citizens that their critical information may be easily stolen because of this bug. The NSA is opportunistic if nothing else; but who is protecting us from the NSA?

You are now aware of how the Democrats are inserting themselves into our everyday lives. You should also know that England ruled the Colonies using this same method by inserting themselves between everyone and everything and then taxed and controlled. They did the same in India and in most of the other countries over which they ruled. It is not by

12

happenstance that the DemoParty operates in the same manner!

It is quite clear that the DemoParty does not want to govern a free people. They may have lost control of the U.S. Senate to the Republicans; but through the DemoParty White House, they are continuing to insert new rules between everybody and everything. **Remember the old adage, "If you can control a thing, you own a thing"**. They control healthcare insurance, the healthcare industry, the coal industry, the fake celltower your cellphone connects to, the oil industry, the stock market, the air you breathe, all forms of water on your land, the water you drink, the automotive industry, electric utilities, water utilities, and just about everything else of importance in your lives. It is not really a stretch to realize their real goal is to control and rule every aspect of our lives and to spy on those that they don't. This is the challenge we face and one that we must meet and overcome.

CHAPTER 3
Republicans To The Rescue...
Let's See How They Run Congress

As if it wasn't bad enough having the Democrats in charge, in the past the Republicans have been nearly as dangerous; but their tactics were somewhat different. Their fine work was conducted more on the macro level, while the Demolisher Party operates on the micro level.

With the exception of the Reagan years, I do not have many pleasant memories of the Republicans governing our country. They nearly wrecked our financial structure and sold our middle class down the Chinese Drain. Remember the housing bubble created by the Federal Reserve under their watch? Well, that was created to disguise what was really taking place within our economy. The Republicans' path to prosperity was only for big business and it began very quietly.

First, manufacturing was allowed to slowly move off shore as companies sought to take advantage of third world labor rates. As a point of reference, manufacturing is one of the surest ways a country can build real wealth. This was the case for us and is now the case for China. Of course the loss of manufacturing has the opposite effect on the USA. We have become a huge debtor nation; and can you guess which country owns a great deal of our debt? The very one in which American companies are having their products produced.

14

Never mind that China is intent on our destruction. Do you think that we should be concerned about their build-up of armed forces? Do you see a problem with their attempts to widen their sphere of influence? Do you see a problem with them unilaterally increasing the size of their patrolled area of the South China Sea? Do you see a problem with them using our money to do this? Of course, China's new wealth is creating a growing economy. They are building up a middle class as we are destroying ours. Now, they need our natural resources. It should not be surprising to learn that they are now buying up our gas and oil fields or that we are exporting to them refined diesel fuel with the resulting effect of very high diesel fuel prices for us. In fact, our consumption of refined petroleum products has gone down, but our prices have gone up. They have gone up because we are shipping diesel fuel to China. In fact, the touted increase in our domestic manufacturing is mostly due to our refining of oil into diesel fuel. Diesel fuel is one of our top exports and is the reason domestic prices are high.

So as you can see, the Republicans and the Destroyers are cooperating in selling our country's resources out beneath our feet. They think that the Chinese can make better use of our nonrenewable resources than us. Here is one more thumb in the eye of every working man in this country, as many of us drive a diesel truck. As a result, we are paying a higher price for our fuel and so are you, as everything shipped uses this fuel. We are all paying more because we sell diesel fuel to the Chinese. I would prefer that the Chinese pay more and we pay less!

What's more, the Republicans and the Demolishers are also allowing the Chinese to buy our companies; and not just any companies. China has recently been allowed to buy our largest pork producer. Of course, it is supported by our leaders. Do they know that China cannot even produce safe baby food? I know that I sleep well at night knowing that the Chinese would never harm our food supply. Oh, oh, just by coincidence, Porcine Epidemic Diarrhea virus (Pig Flu) was found in the U.S. during the second quarter of 2013; just about the time they were exploring all the company's pig farms. Since that time, this very contagious disease has claimed millions of pigs. What does that tell you about food safety and the Chinese?

There is much more. The Chinese are now one of the biggest land owners in the U.S. and no one is telling you about it; not the DemoPress, not the DemoParty, not the Republicans; even the Conservatives in Congress are not telling you. China does not reciprocate, as their government maintains close control over foreign investments, most of which must directly involve government ownership. Our government is all too keen to sell anything to the Communist Chinese. I am concerned, but I guess that is just me.

The Establishment Republicans have been supporting the Chamber of Commerce's need to replace most of our remaining domestic workers with cheap foreign workers; not

16

foreign workers on foreign soil, but foreign workers on our soil. But alas, the DemoPresident has beaten them to the punch. He is giving executive amnesty to over five million illegals, many of whom will be allowed to become U.S. Citizens. So now, all these new workers will need more and more federally supported social aid. That will make the DemoParty happy! Will these burdensome social costs be paid by the business community? No! The U.S. Citizen will pick up these costs, just like we were made to pick up the bankers' financial losses along with the General Motor and Chrysler bailouts. So, as you can see the Democrats get a permanent lower class that will always vote for them and the Republicans are not really that upset with the President's actions, as it addresses the wants of the business community. So in reality, it's both parties against the U.S. Citizen. Isn't it refreshing to find that they are working together for the benefit of the foreign citizen? I just wish they were working together for the benefit of the U.S. Citizen!

To give you a better idea of where the Republicans stand on the illegal immigrant issue, a Republican politician recently made the claim that these poor illegal aliens are victims and that the laws they are breaking are really just minor infractions. I think his last name may have been Bush? Is he covering up for what his brother and father have done to us by making it appear that the illegals are the victims?

Having a nation without borders allows for this type of thinking and like it or not, that is what we are. Crossing our

17

borders illegally is only a minor infraction when you hear them talk. But to me, I liken it to running a red light. If there are no automobiles in the cross traffic, then there is no real harm; but unfortunately, the U.S. Citizen is in the other car and the illegals are smashing us! I have a big problem with this! I want to know, what team are these two parties on? They are not on the team of the U.S. Citizen!

So allow me to sum it all up for you. We lost our manufacturing base along with all of the supporting jobs; we are selling our nonrenewable resources to China; we are selling our companies to China; we are selling our land and other properties to China and we are importing foreign replacement workers to take our place at home. And all the while, our politicians are telling us that they are so concerned about us and that they want to help us. I think they are helping us right on to skid row! Therefore, the only measure that should be used to judge how well the new Republican majority runs our Congress is to see if they are squarely behind the U.S. Citizen, or squarely behind their special interest supporters.

CHAPTER 4

The DemoParty's Solution To A Weak Economy

The DemoParty wants to raise the minimum wage for all the hourly workers. Now that will produce a lot more jobs! They have also figured out that it isn't jobs that we need, it is a dramatic increase in the supply of U.S. Dollars. So, the Federal Reserve has been printing and printing and printing. (Actually, they do it digitally, but it is the same thing.) And behold, they have driven the stock market to all time highs! Since the USA can no longer create wealth and prosperity for the middle class, we print dollars instead. Of course the money is not being sent to us, rather it is being sent to the bankers. You and I know that the bankers need it much more than us. But alas, the money given to the bankers is not for lending, but for investing. That is their grand answer to all of our economic woes! Just keep printing! And what do you know? There is no inflation! Well, maybe there is a little, but it is only in the things that we buy every day; but those items are not included in their inflation reports. It's great to be in charge of the reports that measure your own work! Like being a student who always gets A's because he is also in charge of grading his own work.

But we, the Wal-Mart shoppers, are living a very different reality. Let us take a look at a very simple item. How about the Oreo Cookie? What has happened to the Oreo

Cookie? It's America's favorite cookie! How could anything be wrong with that? Well, the company has been removing a few cookies from the package every year, while at the same time increasing the price. They are doing the same with their Chips Ahoy brand and most of their other brands as well. And so is every other consumer company; just take a look at toothpaste, an average tube is now half the size it was just a few years ago.

The car companies and insurance companies are raising prices; so are the tire companies and the carpet companies. Just about everything you buy has gone up in price. Rent for living space (apartment or home) has gone up dramatically. The only thing that is going up for you is your workload. But remember, there is no inflation!

I have a simple formula for measuring inflation. It consists of three questions. The answers to these questions will provide you with the severity of the increase in inflation.

1. Are you paying more for the same?

2. Are you getting less and paying the same?

3. Are you paying more for even less?

The correct answer today is the last one. We are all paying much more for even less. Look at diesel fuel prices, we are using less and paying more. Look at the automobile, less steel, smaller tires, less room, less safe, and all that for a higher price. I love downsizing!

Another troubling factor resulting from the Federal Reserve's action is their interference in our stock market.

Companies are not investing money in order to hire more People; they are not investing in their own infrastructure; they are not investing in research and development; they are not building their brands; rather, they are buying back more and more of their own stock. As the number of outstanding shares is reduced, even flat earnings will produce an increase in the profit per share; not because there is more profit, but because there are less outstanding shares. So, the price of the stock goes up. And in this very perverse world produced by the Federal Reserve, if a company announces a restructuring that reduces head count and therefore reduces overhead costs, the stock price really goes up. You got it? The more our companies fire their workers, the higher the stock price goes up, which means that the business executives are financially rewarded for increasing our unemployment rate. Of course, they may hire more part time workers at a much lower salary. But guess what? The DemoParty counts part time workers the same as full time workers. They exclude those workers who are discouraged and quit looking for a job; so the unemployment rate goes down as companies' fire full time workers and switch to part time workers. What difference does it make that earned income is taking a nose dive? The DemoParty can claim unemployment is going down. Victory at last!

In short, the Federal Reserve and the DemoParty have created a fairyland world, where the higher the stock market rises, the more the middle class suffers. **It is apparent to me**

21

that the DemoParty wants to downsize our lives while they super-size their form of government.

CHAPTER 5
What It Means To Be A Conservative

For me, a Conservative is someone who strives to preserve and improve our way of life; our values, our freedoms and our liberties. They are dedicated to improving our economic opportunities. The DemoPress would have you believe that Conservatives represent only the rich and big business and of course, they hate women. But for me, nothing could be further from the truth. A real Conservative is and always has been a champion of the U.S. Citizen. Our country needs someone who will ignite domestic job growth and ignite growth in capital formation; someone who respects the rule of law, someone who knows that when you are elected to represent others, life is no longer about you.

A Conservative will not compel you to do things that are not in your best interest, nor attempt to micro manage your life. A Conservative will do their best to enable you to live a better life. They will not throw up road blocks nor regulate your life or your livelihood away.

The Liberals and Progressives also have their own version of a Conservative. They just prefer to change the name a little and of course, their focus is not on you or me but rather something else. Their version of a Conservative is a conservationist. These individuals are focused on improving the environment and the lives of animals. They elevate the fertilized egg of a turtle above the fertilized egg of a human. They strive to improve the lives of animals. Yes, it is important to be a good shepherd to all animals, but I think it is an upside down world when the DemoParty always elevates the animals' and insects' needs above the needs of our U.S. Citizens. To drive my point home, the DemoParty is using the Endangered Species Act like a club to micro manage us and use it as another means to control us and make us comply. Conversely, a Conservative Conservationist knows it is important to keep a balance between the interests of man and animal.

Nobody Likes Conservatives

Everyone is against the Conservative. The Republican Establishment is against them, the DemoParty says they are mean and selfish and the DemoPress parrots these views and writes about how mean and nasty they are. They pollute our water and our air. They hate all old people and in particular old women. In fact, they hate all women! How can they ever be elected? They are the villains of the political world. Or are they?

If you are a Conservative, you are most likely a Republican. But the Establishment Republicans detest you along with any neighborhood groups that support you. How can a Conservative ever succeed, let alone win the Republican nomination and then the general election?

But what have Establishment Republicans come up with to fight against the DemoParty's YWC policies? Nullification! Now there is a great idea! Let's just keep voting to strike down ObamaCare. Further, let's do everything we can to block everything. Why do they wonder they are called the party of "No"? What else is in their bag of election strategy? Hope. Hope that ObamaCare fails and the voters will continue to turn toward the Republicans. They believe voters will hold their noses and vote for the Republicans in 2016 just like they did in 2014. They are counting on the voters to be fed-up with the Demolishers in the White House.

25

Of course, the voters will not hear any new ideas from the Republicans, but they will be angrier with the Demolishers then they are with the Republicans, so they will vote Republican. Maybe? Maybe not?

True to their nature, the Establishment Republicans will always take the safe road. They will not initiate any bold programs or do the heavy lifting that is required to get this country headed in the right direction. Keep in mind, that they must keep the Chamber of Commerce happy. So, they will do what they do every four years; manage the nomination process. Just like always, they will work hard to insure that a middle-of-the-road Presidential candidate will be nominated. You see, they want to appeal to the moderate Democrats and the Independents. This strategy has always worked so well in the past! They may even nominate another Bush. (We need another Bush like we need another Clinton!) The big daring move they could make is to nominate the governor from New Jersey; but his staff was more like the DemoParty, wielding power to punish those who do not comply. That Bridgegate thing was right out of a Democrat play book! But alas, he is not the answer either. It is an unsolved mystery why the Republicans do not know that doing the same thing over and over again will only produce the same results over and over. Do they really want to win the popular vote? I wonder.

Why do we need another Republican nominee that has one foot in the Democrat Party? Do these people still believe they can cross the isle and shake hands with John Podesta and

26

Harry Reid? The hands we want to shake belong to the rank and file Democrats, Libertarians, Republicans and Conservatives.

So, how can a real Conservative fight his way through all of this? I grant you, it will be a difficult task but not impossible. Besides, our citizens love to see the little guy taking on the big political machines? Heck, you only need to convenience about 130 million people. Sounds simple doesn't it? Well it can be done with the right plan.

CHAPTER 6
The Plan and Play Book

First, Conservatives need to have a clear understanding of the priorities that will have the broadest appeal to the U.S. Citizens. Is immigration the leading voter concern? Is it global warming? How about women's issues? Is it student loans? In my mind, it is none of these. These are the issues that the DemoParty uses to divide us. These are not the broad based issues that will unite us. The DemoParty wants to divide us and distract us. A Conservative must focus on the issues that bring us together. **The single most important issue is Trust!** The U.S. Citizen wants to vote for someone they trust. They have a very low opinion of Congress and the President's trust numbers are sinking. Trust is first and foremost.

Second, be on the side of the U.S. Citizen. They are longing to find someone who will be honest with them and will place their interests above the special interest.

Third, have a concrete plan that will produce quality jobs, not part time jobs. I fear that the new Republican majority in Congress will want to reduce corporate taxes with the hope that the corporations will add a few new jobs in return. That is not negotiating, that is capitulating. Nor should they reduce corporate taxes as a payback for campaign contributions. That is just politics as usual. We learned the real cost of that with the DemoParty's Solyndra deal. The path

28

I recommend does not leave that to chance; corporations will be required to earn any tax cuts as you will soon read.

Fourth, make an ironclad offer of an honest government.

Fifth, get government out of the business of regulating our lives on a micro level and solve the overreaching bureaucracy problem once and for all.

Sixth, all your actions if elected will focus on enhancing the lives of all U.S. Citizens.

Seventh, solve the real problems, not the symptoms. High taxes are a symptom. High social costs are a symptom. High unemployment is a symptom. A lower standard of living is a symptom. The problem is the current economic environment in the USA. We need to build an economic environment for the benefit of all U.S. Citizens. We need to develop a wealth building environment, not just for Wall Street but for Main Street. And then our government needs to get out of the way.

I am proposing ten planks that focus on improving the lives of the U.S. Citizen. Together they make a Conservative Platform that is capable of winning the 2016 Presidential Election. It will win because it focuses on the real issues. It will win because it crosses party lines and unites us as a people. It is the true embodiment of Reagan's big tent. It will not be welcomed by the Democrat or Republican Party Leaders. It will not be welcomed by our national press or the business community or the lobbyists. These folks are heavily invested in the status quo and they will only support these planks after they garner some level of popular support; and even then it will be limited and grudgingly offered. These forces are considerably strong and they will fight you at every turn. They will launch a series of ever intensified personal attacks against your character; all funded by seemingly unlimited financial support from the entrenched power brokers. Conservatives had better be thick skinned and have a firm grip on their principals. They will do their best to create doubts about you in the minds of our voter. Fortunately, this platform is capable of generating the unwavering support of many of our U.S. Citizens.

Again, the U.S. Citizens are our core constituency. These ideas do not advantage any splinter group or any singular group of Conservatives, Moderates, Liberals, Progressives or Libertarians.

This is our country, our government. Our Constitution does not begin with "We the business community" or "We the environmentalists" or "We the lobbyists" or "We the government bureaucrat" or "We the Democrats" or "We the Republicans". It begins with "We the People of the United States". Simply put, they are the focus of this plan.

The Tea Party has experienced some setbacks in recent primaries for one main reason. They have failed to lay out a comprehensive and inclusive plan. As a consequence, they are portrayed as only being concerned about spending and taxes. One issue platforms do little to excite the voter.

30

This plan is inclusive and offers bold solutions to key voter issues. Its main goal is to enhance the lives of all our U.S. Citizens.

Please note, that I do not call our country "America" nor do I call our citizens "Americans". "Americans" is the word Liberals and the DemoParty use to refer to all citizens of North, Central and South America. For them, they are all Americans. So to be clear, the U.S. Citizens and their welfare is the singular focus of this work. A further note, this is not a populist plan, it does not offer financial incentives for votes. It offers more economic opportunities to all and if implemented it provides for a more honest, a more restrained government playing a more limited role in our daily lives.

CHAPTER 7
Where There Is Smoke There Is Fire

Shame, shame and more shame! Is there no one in Washington D.C. who even knows what this word means? Do they ever feel a little twinge of conscience when they say one thing and then do something else entirely? What kind of person can look the U.S. Citizen in the eye and tell them over and over an out-and-out lie? Or what about the ones who cleverly muddy up the facts and call it "spin"? Unfortunately, they are able to compartmentalize their conscience in such a way that they can lie on the one hand and think it justified on the other. I do not remember being taught that deceit is the best path to follow to win the U.S. Citizens' hearts and minds. Be assured these liars sleep well at night; they have crossed the line so many times, the line no longer exists. And what an example for society! Do these politicians not know that their lies are leading to a complete breakdown of trust in our government? And yes, Madam Secretary of State it does matter!

It is illegal for us to lie to Congress or to the FBI and don't even try to lie to the IRS. Like most other things, the rules only apply to us and not to our betters in Washington D.C. They can lie with immunity. We get fined and sent to jail! **We need to let them know that their pants are on fire!**

32

The Conservative Solution
Plank One
Make It Illegal For Government Officials
To Lie To The U.S. Citizens

Not every statement or comment needs to be truthful; but there are some statements that must be honest and true. This law would take into account the difference.

This law would apply to all elected officials in our federal government. It would also apply to any individual holding an office that requires Senate approval along with their department personnel; including their press secretaries and any other official speaking for these departments. It also applies to all published reports issued by these same departments; which include the State Department, the Defense Department, the EPA, and the Department of Education and so on. Verbal statements will fall under the purview of this law only when and if they are identified as "Official Statements".

The punishment for lying to the U.S. Citizens will be the same as it is for lying to the FBI, and must be adjudicated in a similar manner.

For example, when a Secretary of State makes a speech about the facts leading up to, during and after a critical incident in which U.S. Citizens have been killed and she/he does not label the statement as an "Official Statement", then you can assume that it is something other than the truth. If on the other hand, she/he does identify the statement as an "Official Statement", then it had better be the truth, the whole truth and nothing but the truth.

Similarly, during a town meeting or when conducting a live web chat conference, our elected officials do not need to tag any statement with the words "Official Statement". The law applies only to statements claiming to be "Official Statements". As a practical matter, participants may inquire if something the politician said is an "Official Statement", if the answer is in the affirmative, the law applies. If the answer is "No", then again you can assume that it is something less than the truth.

The same will apply to press conferences. Any member of the participating press may ask the politician or government official giving the press conference if any of his/her statements are "Official Statements".

Let us not forget the various reports issued by our government. A good example is the Jobs Report. Presently, this report focuses on the headline number, but that is deceiving and misleading. The real number is the U-6 portion of the report. The U-6 includes the total unemployed plus total part time as a percent of all the civilian labor pool. This number is the real unemployment number. That number averaged over 13% in 2013. They do not want you to focus on this number as you may realize that the U.S. still has a significant unemployment problem. This law would require honest reporting.

How about the Consumer Price Index Report? This one has been manipulated until it shows the most favorable report for the money printing Federal Reserve. How about including all items like food and fuel that consumers buy on a regular basis and keep the items measured constant for a 12 month period. When measuring food, measure the same items and do not assume that the consumer is switching to something cheaper. This report will also need to be amended if we mandate honest reporting from our government.

There is no downside to this idea from the U.S. Citizen's point-of-view. It crosses the isle, includes all races, all nationalities, and all religions. The Progressives will love it. The Conservatives will love it. The Moderates will love it. Even the press will love it! And it directly addresses the TRUST FACTOR.

It's a pity that we have come to this, but whom in their right mind wants to hear any more lies out of the mouths of our elected officials? Their actions have led us to this point. We have a basic and fundamental right to have an honest government and honest politicians. ***Lies that hide a political party's ulterior motives and secret agendas undermine and corrupt a government of 'We the People'.***

CHAPTER 8
The Super Citizens and You

Many Americans are suffering from an income gap which is creating a wealth gap. The good news is our President has a fix; he wants to increase the minimum wage. All of his supporters laude his efforts and feel encouraged that, yes, he is the great problem solver for the middle class. Really? That's all that needs to be done? Just raise the minimum wage? Why didn't we do that before? We can all relax because the new jobs are just around the corner. Prosperity will come flowing to the middle class and we will all enjoy our new jobs and our new found wealth. This one must have taken all of at least 3 minutes to think up!

Here is a real shocker for you. The income gap is not the problem. It is the symptom brought about by the real problems. There are five areas that are causing the wealth gap to regain its all time historical highs. But do not hold your breath waiting for the President to identify any of these areas. And don't wait for any of the Democrats or the Republicans to inform you either. Well, should we just give up and settle for a higher minimum wage? No! What we must do is identify and solve the underlying factors that are producing this income/wealth gap.

The Foundational cause of the Income/Wealth Gap is Entré

You see, in the real world of politics there are people who have power and need money and there are other people who have money and need someone with influence; like a good friend in high political office. If you think about it, it makes for a perfect marriage of money and power. One can provide the money the politician needs for the next election and the other can smooth the path for you and your company to make even more money. Need to lower your labor costs? Let's move your business offshore. Now, give me the financial support I need for my next campaign or maybe just a nice profitable speaking tour after I retire. Just ask Hillary how much Goldman Sachs paid her for just two such speeches (about $400,000). They did this because they see her as an investment. I cannot imagine why a leading bank would want to invest in her. Can you think of any reason? It may be they want to name her the "Queen of Goldman Sachs".

This practice is as old as civilization itself, but it did not gain a foothold in the U.S. until the end of the Civil War. At that time Reconstruction was getting into full gear, so the time was right to ask for a few favors. Many of those favors were asked for and granted in the lobby of the Willard Hotel in Washington D.C. That is where President Grant would occasionally relax with a drink and a cigar. These visits to the hotel became well known and men seeking political favors or federal contracts would seek him out in the lobby of the hotel.

37

It is uncertain if this is the origin of the term "Lobbyist", but one thing is for sure, the practice of lobbying succeeded beyond their dreams. From that humble beginning, the lobbying industry has developed and grown. All it took was a strong federal government, lots of tax money and a little give and take; one gives money and the other takes it. And coincidentally, the USA has been the world's largest economy since Grant's days in office but as of the end of 2014, China is now the largest economy. Do you think that the lobbyists and money men had a hand in this change of leadership? They and their compliant politicians most certainly had a lot to do with this change.

This powerhouse alliance between our politicians and their money men is moving full steam ahead, as the more successful lobbying firms have smartly hired former congressmen and well placed government officials, because they have all those nice close connections with those still in Congress and in various government departments. Lobbying on steroids! What a winner!

So, back to income inequality; it is here and it is growing. In fact, the width of the gap between the haves and the have-nots is back at the historical highs of the 1910's and the 1920's. Those were the years of the Robber Barons and the Steel Tycoons. Back then the tycoons held great sway over our politicians. Then along came a Republican by the name of Teddy Roosevelt who took a keen interest in the ubber-rich. He focused on trust busting and regulating big business. He fought the Republicans of his day along with the upper 1% of our population and his image ended up on Mount Rushmore. There is room for one more!

Over the many decades following Teddy Roosevelt's actions, a strong middle class emerged as the U.S. economy expanded and the demand for workers grew. Much of this dynamic growth happened during the post World War I and II periods.

The unions also played a key role during this time frame. Among their many contributions was the 40 hour work week and the creation and expansion of company sponsored healthcare programs and retirement programs. But as often happens over time, the unions became too powerful, greedy and demanding. Even large organizations need to know their limitation; their own hubris caused their ranks to shrink. They found out that business managers will not let the unions run their business into the ground. They moved offshore!

You may have surmised by now that the cause of our malady is not the wage gap, but the influence gap. The lobbyists, wealthy individuals, large financial institutions, unions, companies and organizations are what I call the "SuperCitizens". They have direct access to our politicians. I call it "entré". Their power and money allows them to meet with our politicians at any time and place. Unfortunately, these meetings have had a catastrophic effect on the rest of us. We do not have the money or the influence and we will never have it. We are left out in the cold and ignorant of what is taking place during these meetings.

I would very much like to hear our President's opinion regarding the influence gap. I would also like to hear the answer from all the DemoParty leaders as well as the Establishment Republicans. I will bet that they will avoid answering that question. They will not want to be asked about the influence gap. I doubt that anyone from the DemoPress will even pose a question about the influence gap.

The influence gap is the foundational reason we have a wage gap and a wealth gap; it has nothing to do with the minimum wage. There are five major factors which have caused this gap and I will detail each of them in this book, but it starts with entré.

You may ask what is wrong with these individuals and groups meeting with our politicians. After all, they are citizens too. Frankly, there is nothing wrong with these meetings or with these groups financially helping our politicians to get reelected. In fact, the Supreme Court has made the case that the giving of money to support a candidate is a form of free speech and they let stand the current financial contribution limits one can give to an individual candidate. So, money is not the problem and the meeting is not the problem, what is the problem? The problem is that these meetings are conducted in secret and what is being said and what is being planned is kept secret. What don't they want us to know? What would they be planning in secret? Are they planning something that is not

40

in our best interest? The real problem is money men and elected officials or their aides meeting in secret. Freedom and liberty die behind locked doors where money men and public servants are meeting in secret!

An in-your-face example of these meetings occurred just before the last Presidential Election. Our President had several of his aids meet with lobbyists and financial supporters, not in the White House where their names would be logged by the Secret Service; rather they were held nearby at Jackson Place, away from prying eyes and ears. Why would he want this? He is a public official and surely he would want us to know that these meetings were in the U.S. Citizen's best interest; or were they? These meetings must have been so toxic to the U.S. Citizen that he did not even want their names to be known. Sadly, he was only following the same practice used by Bush, Clinton and Bush 2. How do you think the banks got their bailouts or how do you think the automotive unions got their bailouts? How do you think Chrysler, a privately held company, got its bailout? How do you think businesses were allowed to move their manufacturing offshore? How do you think every major costly program was ever created, planned and artfully executed upon an unsuspecting U.S. Citizen? Why do you think new oil drilling leases on federal land are not being approved? Think of any recent federal law or regulation and you will find a special interest group behind it. In fact, it has risen to such a level that the lobbyists and special interest

41

folks are actually writing most of the text of proposed new bills.

Now we have unelected special interest groups doing the work of our elected officials. The healthcare companies and their lobbying organizations were writing the ObamaCare law. Are you surprised to learn that the healthcare companies are making money hand-over-fist after this law was enacted? The same holds true for the bankers, as they and their lobbyists wrote the portion of the new *cromnibus spending bill* that relaxed banking regulations.

The Chrysler bailout is the best and the worst example of how these meetings and relationships can cost us big. Chrysler was 80% owned by a private finance group called Cerberus Capital Management. This is a privately owned company that obtained bailout money from the government. I don't care what the agreements were, this is a private company and we had to help them with Chrysler? How many other private companies has the Federal Government bailed out? None that I know of! So, that makes this one unique.

It is by design that Cerberus has a long practice of hiring former politicians with terrific connections in the White House and in Congress. It seems to have paid off big for them. They are very well connected. I would not be surprised to learn that a lot of very well known current and past politicians are invested in this company.

If all these meetings were made public, our citizens would be outraged and few, if any, of these special favors would be approved. The public would not stand for these shenanigans. So, they are conducted in secret. The results of these meetings are then carefully crafted and professionally presented to an uninformed public. Or worse yet, they are never presented; rather they are carefully and artfully implemented.

These meetings are successful because they are conducted in secret. They have resulted in moving jobs offshore; giving tax dollars to failing, privately owned companies; moving banking loses to the taxpayer while allowing the bankers to keep the profits for themselves; killing the coal industry and the related jobs including the transportation industry that moves the coal, all the while passing costs on to the public. All of this and more they can do because these meetings are conducted in secret in the back room. Our government belongs to these Oligarchs; it is they who really rule our country. **It is time for us to remind them all that we are a self-governing people; we rule not them!**

The Conservative Solution
Plank Two
Use the NSA To Record These Meetings
and Make Them Public

Earlier I wrote that the Democrats are intent on coming between everyone and everything and then controlling us on a micro level. It is time we learned to use this contrivance for the good of our citizens.

I propose to place the U.S. Citizen between the politician and their money men. It is time for us to require our politicians to place the U.S. Citizen first; not the wealthy, the special interests, the corporations and all their lobbyists. We have every right to know what is being said between our politicians and these special interest groups. Yes, they have a right to privacy but not secret speech where money meets power. This is where freedoms come to die.

I propose that every meeting between our politicians and these special interest groups or individual money men be recorded and published on the web within 24 hours.

The NSA has clearly demonstrated that they have the power to record everything we write and say, so let's turn them into an asset for the U.S. Citizen. We must use them to protect our liberty and freedom and to wrestle the power away from the lobbyist and special interest groups.

Since the nature of these meetings can be ad hoc, a NSA phone app can be developed and placed on every politician's

44

cell phone and the phones of all their staffers and family members. In that way, the NSA will be able to record these conversations anywhere, anyplace and at any time. As well, any other conceivable recording device can and should be used to ensure that these meetings are recorded and made public along with any preceding and proceeding written correspondence between the parties. Further, this law is to apply only to our federally elected officials and their staff and immediate families. While they may represent only one side of the equation, it is they who are elected to represent us and it is they who are accountable to the U.S. Citizen; therefore, it is they who must now comply!

There will be exceptions to this rule. Meetings with companies working on various secret projects will be exempt. Meetings with any group or organization whose sole purpose is to defend our constitutional rights will be exempt. (I am quite sure that our politicians can think of many more exceptions.)

I realize that we cannot control the hoards that work for the Oligarchs; but we can and must hold our politicians accountable and personally responsible. Therefore, the law must carry an appropriate penalty for those who wish to continue to conduct secret meetings. I propose that a first offense deserves a hand slap and an "Official Statement" in writing must be produced by the offending parties detailing the meeting. (This will fall under the purview of my first proposal.) Any second offence will be a felony.

Our government knows the value of the NSA and their ability to spy on us. We also know the value of the NSA and we need to turn them around and use the NSA to ensure our politicians are doing the right things for the U.S. Citizens.

With the exceptions pointed out above, I cannot think of one good reason why these meetings should be conducted in secret. Conversely, there are many good reasons for them not to be conducted in secret.

Every politician that lives and breathes will fight this rule. They will do everything within their power to prevent this from becoming a law. Success will depend upon an informed voting public.

I realize that anything even close to this idea will be challenged in Federal Court. It is my hope that the Supreme Court will come down on the side of freedom and liberty for the U.S. Citizen. Secret speech between money men and public officials cannot be protected by the U.S. Constitution as it most often results in the destruction of our middle class!

I cannot find any downside to this proposal for our U.S. Citizen. It is a win for freedom and liberty! It is a win for rank and file Conservatives, Liberals, Libertarians, minorities and religious groups. I remind you, that socialism does not survive in an open environment. Corruption does not survive in an open environment. Special advantages do not survive in an open environment. Conversely, Freedom and Liberty grow in an open and honest environment.

46

So, ask yourself, which side are you on? Are you on the side of the secret deals with money men or on the side of revealing what is being said in these meetings between our public officials and these SuperCitizens?

By the way, this law would also protect honest companies and individuals from the corrupt politician, who may be threatening the firms or individuals with severe governmental oversight, if they do not make a significant contribution to their campaign fund. If you are not aware, one of the first things that a new politician is told by his party leaders is he/she will need to spend the majority of their time soliciting campaign contributions. Do you think that they will hesitate to make a few unsolicited phone calls to wealthy constituents?

The Fight Ahead

To win the Republican nomination, a Conservative will need to compete against a well entrenched and powerful leadership. And then, it will be on to the general election against the Democrat's candidate and all of their supporters. There is no doubt that to get this law enacted, it will necessarily entail a number of very key debates during the primaries and then the general election. There will also be a tremendous amount of personal attacks waged by the well entrenched power brokers in Washington D.C. These SuperCitizens will spend untold wealth in order to stop this law. But when all is said and done, it is a fight that we must have and we must win for the sake of our people and our country.

The Citizens of this country will want to see this passed, so thankfully, they will be the ultimate deciders.

Besides, the Conservatives have nothing to lose. The leaders of both political parties do not like you and do not want you to succeed. But we the people, we love to see a fight like this one; a little guy versus the big money guy and the big power guy. My best advice to anyone who champions this cause is to buckle-up and keep in mind the Devil loves a coward.

One last item, for the sake of us all; the writing of bills must be exclusively performed only by our elected officials and their staffs.

CHAPTER 9
Jobs, Jobs, Jobs and More Jobs

All the talking heads on TV and radio are discussing our jobless recovery. The politicians are eager to express their thoughts, but none of them have a plan. They wring their hands and talk. They remind me of Clara Peller; if you're old enough you may remember her as the woman who said in her famous Wendy's ad; "Where's the Beef". In the case of a real jobs program, there is no program; there is no beef!

Not one politician has presented a plan that will get the job done. They do not know what to do, or if they do, they are not doing it. Fine! Conservatives are up to the challenge!

If you are an informed citizen, then you, like me, are aware of the situation in Washington D.C. Congress and the Executive Branch are filled with self serving individuals intent on improving their own lives, not our lives. What was the rationale for our politicians allowing manufacturing jobs to go overseas? It certainly was not in our best interest. It must have been in the politician's best interest. Why did it happen? Worse yet, will they ever want to reverse it and bring the jobs back? If I had to guess, I would say "No".

If these folks are not working for us, they must be working for themselves or for some other special interest. Do you think that they were concerned about giving all of our manufacturing expertise and processes to the Chinese? Again, the answer is "No".

50

Now that they have done their worst, they are all telling us that those meaningful jobs will never return to the USA. They tell us to be happy with low wage service jobs and that the best they can do is to raise the minimum wage. They recommend that we go back to school and learn new skills so we can get a high paying tech job. Unfortunately, the tech industry is pushing for an increase in allowing better educated foreigners to come into our country as part of the amnesty/immigration program, so those jobs will not be there either. So what can be done? The Republican answer may be to lower corporate taxes and hope the corporations hire a few more people. To give them a tax cut with no strings attached would be a huge mistake.

Let's take a look at the commercial strength within the USA. What can we best leverage within the world community so the U.S. can grow jobs? At present we do not leverage anything. In fact, our politicians are diminishing any advantages we may have as they do not even recognize that our country has borders. No borders, no protection for what remains of our U.S. Workers. Without borders, our U.S. Citizens are forced to compete with every low wage worker who sneaks over our southern border. It always comes back to the same old question, who are these politicians working for; the citizens of the world or the U.S. Citizen?

But we do have a real strength; a hidden strength that we do not leverage to gain an advantage. What is it that the U.S. has that every foreign company wants? How can we use this strength to improve job growth for our U.S. Citizens? How can we use this strength to grow our economy? How can we improve our balance of trade at the same time? How can anything we have offer solutions to more than one of our problems?

Well, this will surprise you; but one of our biggest weaknesses can also become our biggest strength. Our weakness is that we are addicted to consuming. We buy and then we buy more and still more. We max out our credit cards and still we want to buy. In fact, over 70% of our entire Gross Domestic Product is driven by consumers and it has produced the biggest economy in the world. Every foreign and domestic company is anxious to grab a bigger and bigger piece of the U.S. Consumer. The problem is that none of these manufacturers want to invest in the U.S. worker; they prefer to use low wage foreign labor, sell the goods to us and then take the money back to their home countries. That money leaves the USA. It circulates within their country and builds their economy; it is not circulated here to expand our own economy.

But let's look at the U.S. Consumer from a different angle. In reality, our ability to consume is our greatest strength. We keep the world's companies producing and producing. Think of all the jobs we create on a global basis.

52

What power! I believe we must use this strength to our advantage.

High Priced American Labor Versus The World

This may come as a shock to you, but I do not care about the employment numbers in China, India or even Germany. I do care about the USA's employment numbers. Why is that so important to me and to you? Employment gives us dignity and a purpose to life. It gives us a genuine sense of accomplishment. It gives us a real sense of pride. It provides for our children's welfare and education. It allows us to build a nest egg to prepare for an uncertain future or for our retirement. It gives us value; value of self and value of others who work with us. A job gives meaning to our lives. To have real work is a blessing; a blessing to our families and to the community at large. It makes us all better citizens. It brings self satisfaction. Real jobs are what we must strive for and what we must provide, for the good of all of us.

Conversely, not having real work has the opposite effect. It gives us a sense of worthlessness; a loss of self respect and a real sense of hopelessness. It brings about an endless downward spiral that crushes our spirit and destroys families. At all costs, it is to be avoided!

Welfare, unemployment benefits and food stamps are only a safety-net; they are not a solution and they are certainly not a way of life. Social programs serve a short term need but the only acceptable answer is good jobs.

Sometimes, the economic environment is not conductive to job growth. There are down turns in every economy as manufactures over produce and we have too many goods chasing too few dollars. But that is not what has happened to us. **We have downsized our economy on purpose.** We have moved manufacturing overseas and at the same time offered unfettered access to our markets for these same companies. We are moving wealth from our pockets to the pockets of the foreign companies, their foreign workers and their foreign governments. Their economies are growing, their housing market is growing, their automobile market is growing and their military might is growing. Conversely, our job market is shrinking. Therefore, our economy shrinks, our housing market shrinks and our military might shrinks. Is the free world better off with a strong China? Is the free world better off with a weakened America? Is Russia's military conquest on the rise? Did they invade the countries of Georgia and the Ukraine? Do you think that China will come to our aid or the aid of the Russians? Is this producing a better life for our U.S. Citizens or a safer life for our children? Is our standard of living improving? The answer to all of these questions is obvious and yet, nothing is being done to turn this situation around.

Again, I ask, what team are the Democrats and the Republicans on? I think it is team Big Business. Business knows no national borders and if they do exist, they do their best to knock them down. Our politicians endorsed and implemented trade treaties that knocked down our borders. (Treaties carry the weight of a statute; but once they are ratified, they can also give the federal government extraordinary powers that sometimes can conflict with our U.S. Constitution.)

In the past, Americans have produced magnificent bridges, dams that produce electricity, cattle ranches, oil fields, wine, fresh produce, meat for our table, concrete for our roads and buildings, clothes, school text books, automobiles, computers and cell phones. We all enjoy the products that our prior generations have produced. Their work has made our lives much easier. They had work because our economy was creating good jobs. Now, we no longer offer meaningful jobs. Why? Because our companies could not compete domestically with products produced by cheap overseas labor after our politicians allowed those overseas companies unfettered access to our markets. So our domestic companies were undermined by cheap foreign products and they could not compete in foreign markets due to higher U.S. production costs. So, they joined the party and moved their plants overseas. They could now compete in both the domestic as well as foreign markets. The flood gates were now wide open and here came the foreign goods. All of this caused the U.S. worker participation to shrink. **We are now producing less with less people working for less money.** Great for business but a disaster for the U.S. Citizen!

All businesses want unfettered access to every customer worldwide and they do not care if it means a weaker USA. Businessmen are paid to improve the bottom line of their company, they are not overly concerned about a country's security or the welfare of its citizens; that is, as long as it does not interfere with business. They will do everything in their power to keep their operating costs low and their profit margins high. The president of any business knows full well the contribution margin of every product and every employee down to the one-hundredth of a percent. They will never willingly do anything that will decrease their employee contribution margin or productivity margin. With a mindset like this, you can clearly understand that giving corporations a tax reduction would do nothing to bring about more jobs. They would gladly take the money with no strings attached and drop it to the bottom line of their Profit and Loss Statement. In short, they would use it to further prop-up their stock price. So, as long as the Republicans are in bed with business, you will never hear them recommend anything that will negatively affect any company's operating margins. As well, you will never hear anything from the DemoParty either. They want a needy U.S. Citizen whom is dependent upon government social programs. A successful citizen has no need of the DemoParty. So once again, both the Democrats and the Republicans are teaming up to prevent prosperity from reentering the middle class in America.

(As a point of reference, I feel it is important to let you know that I worked for over 31 years for an international company. They were a principled company and I was fortunate to have worked for them. I am by no means opposed to big business. But, as strongly as I support them, it cannot be at the expense of our own economy. The world is a better and safer place with a strong USA and that depends upon a strong and successful middle class.)

So, what is replacing work in today's market? Enter the Federal Reserve. The Federal Reserve continues to provide us with a false feeling of prosperity. First, they produced the dot-com bubble; second, came the housing bubble and now we have a stock market bubble. You and I lived through these bubbles and the consequences of their bursting. How many of us felt wealthy because the price of our homes continued to accelerate? What did this false wealth effect produce? We used our houses as an ATM machine. We took out larger and larger mortgages and larger second mortgages. We felt wealthy and we spent money like we really were wealthy. But we were not wealthy; it was just the Federal Reserve pumping the money pump. And what a disaster it proved to be! Many of us lost our homes, which the bankers and other large financial institutions now own. Many of us lost our jobs and the Federal Reserve's actions are only accelerating more job losses. Printing money is not the answer. A near-zero overnight interest rate is not the answer. Jobs are the answer!

But, as I have explained, our politicians do not want to create good jobs!

You might think that with two bubbles blown to bits, that the Federal Reserve would stop blowing bubbles. You would be wrong! The Federal Reserve is not through; no way, no how. In addition to ultra-low interest rates, and printing more and more money, this same bunch has been taking on the bad mortgage loans and buying up all the sub-prime automobile loans that they can get their hands on. All of this they are doing to support their fake economy. By keeping bond rates artificially low, the stock market has become the only place to invest in order to obtain a decent return. The Federal Reserve is again creating a false wealth effect. The professional stock market investor will be getting out at the top, but the retail investor will again be stuck with the loss.

So, rather than provide an economic environment that will create jobs, our politicians talk about increasing the minimum wage while the Federal Reserve prints more money. This has proven to be a losing combination; but, that does not deter them. In reality, the Federal Reserve is manned with illusionists that make it appear we are living in a strong economy and the politicians are busy selling the illusion as reality. Do not be fooled, we are not living in a strong economic environment. The Dow Jones Industrial average was at 7,949 the day Mr. Obama took office. It is now 10,000 points higher and it is still rising. Has our economy grown 226% since that time? Has the global economy grown 226%

during that time? The answer is no! So, is it easy to see that our stock market is totally detached from our real economy? You should also be aware that the stock market will continue to rise as long as the Fed keeps interest rates at a near zero rate. They cannot raise rates without the stock market falling and then it will be the beginning of the end.

As I stated earlier, the Federal Reserve's actions are having an adverse effect upon our economy and upon our country. Businesses are not investing in the growth of their own business but rather they are borrowing money at very low rates and buying back their own stock to make it appear that their profits are growing, when in reality it is the number of outstanding shares that are shrinking. You see, thanks to all the jobs being shipped overseas, there are fewer people working full time jobs and more working part time jobs and that is resulting in lower sales at many of these same companies. Now, to further aid in their quest for more profit, many companies are moving their headquarters overseas to avoid the higher U.S. business taxes. They are able to do this by buying an overseas business and using the overseas business address as their new world headquarters' address. Those U.S. companies remaining here are clamoring for a lower tax rate because the plethora of DemoParty social programs are costing more and more money and there is a growing need for more tax revenue; but businesses do not want to be responsible for any of those expenditures.

The truth is that businesses created all their own woes. Because the jobs went overseas, there was a need for more social programs for the unemployed, and those still working were working for less money and that resulted in the consumer buying less, so the top line (sales revenue) of many businesses has been decreasing. Businesses should be careful what they wish for!

You may think given all of the above, that there would be no reason to add an accelerant to the rate of job losses in the USA. You would be wrong! A Chinese company called Alibaba has been and continues to be the accelerant! This company's main business is to connect Chinese manufacturers along with other foreign manufacturers directly to American companies. That is, through Alibaba's webpage any American company can be directly linked to any global manufacturer, by-passing all American manufacturers. Imagine what this does to our small business manufacturers. Would you be surprised to learn that Alibaba is the new darling of the USA bankers? Would you be surprised to learn that they are the new darling of Wall Street? Would you be surprised to learn that the founder of this company just listed his company's stock in the USA and that he was given the royal treatment when he appeared on the floor of the New York Stock Exchange? Our bankers love him and our brokerage companies love him and our retailers love him and so do our politicians. He is a star and a welcome addition to the new world order.

When all is said and done, the company is expected to be worth more money than IBM, Apple or Microsoft. Oh, and they are also owned in part by the Chinese Communist Party! Surprise! Surprise! Are we insane or what? Are we not the most self- destructive country next to France? Have you heard one negative comment about this company from any political leader in either the DemoParty or the Republican Party? The answer is no!

Let me put it as plainly and bluntly as possible. **This is a War on the U.S. Citizen!** This is a War on our economy! This is a War on our way of life and no one in the DemoParty, the DemoPress or the Republican Party has raised an alarm. Well I am!

The loss of quality jobs is the second main cause of our ever widening wealth gap.

It is time to end this hoax of an economy. It is time to once again create real jobs. No, we cannot place an import duty on all foreign made goods. That will only lead to a trade war and further disaster. It will not create jobs, only hostility from other countries and it would be strongly opposed by the World Trade Organization. (Remember all those treaties!) I believe that we can solve our employment problem and improve by some measure our very unfavorable balance of trade. (That is, we are buying more goods from other countries than they are buying from us.) Our balance of trade problems clearly show the USA is losing wealth and to solve the problem, our politicians have been encouraging the sale

62

of our non-renewable resources to foreign countries. So, now we are selling the real wealth of our country out from under our own feet. The real bedrock economic strength of our country has been our abundant natural resources and now it has come down to selling them as the only way to offset our negative balance of trade? I do not think that selling these resources does us any favors. I want us to husband these resources and keep them available for our exclusive use. They are a key part of our overall long term strength and I will cover their importance to us later on in this book.

I am proposing a simple solution; one that will improve our country's economic environment and will once again bring meaningful employment to our U.S. Citizens.

Conservative Solution
Plank Three
Consumer/Job Ratio

All international and domestic production, manufacturing and assembly companies, both private and public whose products are being consumed in the USA will be required to provide an audited report containing the following:

- Total global business unit sales and dollar sales by country (the dollar sales will be calculated in USD and the exchange rate being used must be applied at one standardized rate per year).
- Total employee headcount by country broken into two major categories; full time salaried employees and full time hourly workers.

We only need to see the total units and total dollars sold on a per country basis. We do not need an individual breakdown of unit and dollar sales. We would only need to see the macro numbers by country.

Each audit must be conducted by an accredited U.S. accounting firm and must be factual in every aspect under penalty of law. The audit will cover the most recent 5 year calendar period. The annual totals for each of these years along with the 5 year rolling average will be provided to our IRS. Failure to comply will bring a stiff financial penalty and continued failure will compound the financial penalty. The

requested information is to be provided no later than April
15th of the first year following the enactment of this law. All
subsequent annual audits will bring the rolling 5 year average
up to date. Failure to comply will result in a fine to be levied
in the form of a sizable and meaningful incremental income
tax.

Based on the 5 year average information, all companies
will be required to adjust their workforce within the U.S. to
mirror their U.S. Sales. The number that will be applied will
be the higher of the two numbers, either unit or dollar sales.
Therefore, if a company is doing 22% of their global business
in the U.S., then they will be required to employ 22% of their
total salaried as well as 22% of their total hourly employees in
the U.S. If after the results of this audit, they have only 5%
employed in the U.S., they will need to increase their U.S.
headcount to 22%. If they have 25% of their headcount
already in the USA then, if they wish, they can reduce it to
22%. In addition, their workforce in the U.S. must consist of a
minimum of 98% U.S. Citizens. The remaining 2% can be
foreign nationals as long as they are in our country legally.
Again, as with the audit request, failure to execute these hiring
guidelines will result in an incremental and substantial income
tax being levied upon these corporations based on the 5 year
audit results.

There will not be any requirement for them to make large
capital expenditures. They will not need to build a plant or an
office building or even a warehouse; that will be their choice.

65

I would anticipate that their capital expenditures will mirror their headcount, but I would not include capital expenditures as part of this law.

This is a simple formula for a very impactful program. It will ensure our labor force will accurately represent what we purchase from every major international and domestic company. This program will provide our citizens with full time work and a brighter future within the new global work environment.

The various global governments where these companies are headquartered will not be able to successfully protest, as the USA will only be requesting our proportionate share of total global employment by company. This proportionate share will be measured by the only fair means of measurement, that is, consumption. **If we consume more, we must employ more**. Every country could easily adapt a similar measure, as it is fair to all. If Germany consumes 10% of a company's products, then they should have 10% of the company's employees working in Germany and so forth for all global countries.

This proposed program is simple and easily explained and understood. Will there be resistance from these companies? Yes, but current employment practices are destroying the USA and cannot be allowed to continue. The USA must rebuild real wealth along with a strong middle class. Corporate profits built upon shifting our wealth to China must cease.

A timeline for the implementation of this program would need to be established, complete with fixed milestones by which progress will be measured and these milestones cannot be capriciously changed by any future head of the Executive Branch. (What comes to mind are the many changes that Obama has unilaterally made to his own healthcare law.)

In addition, there needs to be a favorability factor built into the program for those companies that adapt the hiring practices that are called for in this program. Those companies must receive preferential treatment within the US. First, they should receive a 5% reduction in their corporate tax rate in the second year of the program. They should continue to receive a 5% reduction in each of the following years, as long as they follow the program guidelines, until they reach a 20% permanent income tax rate. They will then receive a USA Seal of Preference.

This SOP designation will first be granted to domestic companies that already meet or exceed the 5 year audit figure regarding headcount and are meeting the 98%/2% employment requirement. It will also be their responsibility to prove that 98% of their employees are U.S. Citizens. Having met these requirements, they will receive a 5% reduction in their tax rate in the first year and so forth until they also reach the 20% tax rate. This will include all small companies' income tax rate; many of which are taxed on the individual income tax rate and this rate will be reduced over time to the same 20% rate.

67

The SOP designation will also be meaningful in two others ways. First, demand side domestic companies will be incented to do business with these companies as described below. Second, these designated companies will receive a preference in all government contracts.

To insure success and a smoother transition to this program, we must also enact a complementary program which will strongly encourage our domestic companies to buy their goods from a company with an SOP designation. This program will encompass the business demand side of the equation. Those companies, whether they are fabricators buying parts from foreign companies or retail stores buying finished goods from an international company, will be required to buy more and more products from companies having a SOP designation. Even companies like Coach or Apple that design their product domestically and have their goods made overseas will be incented to buy from SOP companies.

These demand side companies will be given graduated tax credits during the first three years of this law as they buy 25%, 50%, 75% of their total purchases from these SOP designated companies. When they reach the 75% mark, (also verified through audits) they will also receive the same corporate tax reductions as described above. Conversely, if they choose not to buy from SOP designated companies, then a graduated and proportionate income tax penalty will be applied to these companies as well. They will also be required to meet the 98%/2% employment requirement. In this manner, we will be covering both the production and the demand side of the equation.

As a further incentive, international corporations will be allowed to bring home all of their foreign profits tax free once they gain an SOP designation. That's right; these billions of dollars can be domesticated on a tax free basis with one proviso, that 25% of this money must be spent on job producing capital expenditures within the US. This will mean more construction jobs and more full time jobs. Allowing this money to stay overseas is monumentally stupid! We need to bring it home and let it circulate within our economy.

Regarding the income tax penalty applied to either the producer companies or the demand side companies, all penalty taxes that are collected under this program will not be put into the general fund. The money will immediately be applied to the payment of our national debt. This must be an integral part of the law. In this way, those companies that are causing us the most harm will be those companies that are helping us to pay off our staggering debt. Rather ironic I think!

Regarding the legality of such a program, the Supreme Court has made it perfectly clear in their ObamaCare ruling that our government can tax anyone and any corporation at any time for anything; even when the individual is in a state of repose and not participating in any commercial activity. So, using an incremental income tax to encourage companies to hire U.S. Citizens is perfectly legal. Income taxes are the sole right of each sovereign country; the World Trade Organization

Charter does not give them any authority over a country's income tax laws.

Yes, there will be some higher prices passed on to the U.S. consumer, but it will produce a much healthier economy along with more tax revenue generated by more workers. Social Security and Medicare will also enjoy renewed financial strength due to increased labor participation. This program will also rebuild our leadership position within the global community.

The real beauty of this program is that it changes our economic model from a manufacturing centered economy to a consumer centered economy. It brings real dollars back into our economy rather than foreign economies. Foreign companies will be compelled to add employees in our country based on our consumption of their products. As more people are employed, more consumption will take place. This program will encourage increased consumption which in this case is a very good thing as it will mean more jobs. Remember to keep in mind that over 70% of our economy is driven by consumption. **The more we consume, the more people are employed**. And I didn't even suggest that we need to raise the minimum wage!

For me, this proposal in elegant in its simplicity and it will quickly improve our employment numbers, our economic numbers and the lives of all our U.S. Citizens. At a minimum, this program will either produce new jobs or reduce our debt;

either way it will be a plus over today's economic environment.

The Independents will love it, the rank and file Democrats and Republicans will love it and I should think that the Libertarians will love it, though I am not sure of anything they will like. Most importantly, it is focused on improving the lives of our U.S. Citizens.

One final comment on the importance of enacting this law; the success of our country and our way of life is the product of two very large engines: Freedom and Liberty. But like all engines they need fuel. The fuel they run on is a healthy economy. A healthy economy makes it possible to support infrastructure, repair roads and bridges, provide more support for education and improve our standing in the world. It allows us to keep and maintain a modernized fighting force that will keep our enemies at bay. It will allow us to increase our generosity during disasters both foreign and domestic and much, much more.

Of all countries in the world, it is most important that this one, this one beacon of freedom and liberty, has a very healthy economy. This is our time to act! Let us pass on to the next generation a prosperous country!

CHAPTER 10
We Are No Longer A Democratic Republic

Our system of government is a representative democracy which means that the majority does not always get their way. Our elected officials are placed in office to represent our interests and it is they who vote on various bills. We have a lower and an upper house in Congress. Each member of the lower house must run for reelection every two years, which is why the House of Representatives is called the People's House, as they reflect the changing minds of the public at large. The upper house, the Senate, is a more deliberative body as their members are elected for six year terms. Therefore, the upper house better represents the minority as the face of its members change at a slower pace. Regardless of their differences, all members of both houses are directly elected by the U.S. Citizens.

Our President is the only member of the Executive Branch who is directly elected by U.S. Citizens. His Cabinet Secretaries and his judicial picks along with a few other and lesser known positions must be approved by the U.S. Senate. This process is one of the few constraints that Congress can place upon our Executive Branch.

All in all, our system of government works and has worked well for over 225 years. But for the past 30 years there is a malignancy growing in our government. This malignancy is growing because our elected officials have passed enormous power to people who are unaccountable to the electorate and their ascendancy to these positions of power does not require Senate approval. What is even more shocking, these folks are given virtual lifetime positions.

In summary, they are not accountable to the U.S. Citizen, have lifetime jobs, write capricious rules and regulations and then they enforce them. Now for the test question: can you name three or more of these individuals? Now do you understand the problem?

The Constitution gives the power to create bills to Congress and the power to sign them into law and execute them to the Executive Branch. This bunch has the power to do both. They enact and then they enforce their own laws and you do not even know their names.

So, what we have is a government within our government that rules with totalitarian authority and very few Congressional constraints. They remain for the most part unknown and unfettered, with the ability to expand laws that bind us and the power to enforce laws that constrain and control us.

Why has no one, not our elected officials nor the DemoPress raised an alarm? How can these people rule our lives with little to no constraints? The question is what can be done about it.

This government within our government is the body of bureaucrats within the various departments of the Executive

Branch. They have been given by Congress the ability to write any and all rules and regulations that carry the weight of law. These bureaucrats issue something called a proposal, under the guise of a trial balloon. They state that these proposals are open to public opinion and comments from Congress, but in reality, they very rarely take these comments into consideration and these bureaucrats do whatever they please. They are insulated from the wrath of the public and Congress. They operate in a vacuum, totally unfettered and for all practical purposes, they have lifetime jobs. In addition, they have a very sympathetic ear within the judicial system which is compromised of like thinking people. These compliant judges have actively expanded the authority of these bureaucrats to rule our lives. Individual freedom and liberty do not enter into the minds of these judges; only control over the populace is important. And guess what? These bureaucrats are busy finding new areas of our lives to control and they do it with enthusiasm! It is time to constrain these bureaucrats and remind them that this is a government of the people.

By intent or through laziness, Congress has not maintained approval authority over all regulations and rules. (In some instances Congress does have the authority to disapprove proposed regulations, but even in these instances where they do have authority, they have rarely acted.) Today, when a bill is signed into law, Congress washes its hands and leaves the rule writing to these same bureaucrats and their compliant judges. The law now takes on a life of its own

74

within the Executive Branch. Often, the real limitations written into the law are ignored and the bureaucrats within the Executive Branch go into areas far beyond the laws intended limitations. I blame Congress. They have capitulated and given total control of rule making to the bureaucrats.

In fact, before the 2014 mid-term elections, the DemoParty in the Senate had rewritten the Senate rules in order to further these same bureaucrats' ability to write any regulation they wish. The Senate, under "Reid the Wrecker", disabled any minority advantages in the U.S. Senate in order to pack the D.C. Court with compliant judges. That court has jurisdiction over these very same bureaucrats and their new rules. So, now they not only have a green light to destroy our freedoms, but have been given jet fuel to speed up our demise. The DemoParty has every reason to love "Reid the Wrecker", the great demolisher of our freedoms and liberty. Now the EPA, the IRS and Homeland Security can treat us like ants under a microscope. And you ask, what about the DemoPress? They are the cheerleaders on the sidelines encouraging the DemoParty to do more, to regulate job growth into the grave and to quell any and all decent. It is time for us to act!

The Conservative Solution
Plank Four
Part 1
Congress Is The Only Elected Body
Enabled To Approve Regulations

The Constitution does not grant the power of writing laws to the Executive Branch. But, Congress has written and passed many laws that leave a great deal of leeway for the Executive Branch to write their own rules. Without question, these rules/regulations smell like laws, look like laws and carry the weight of laws; rules by any other name are still laws. The Affordable Care Act is a great example of how Congress gives the bureaucrats very wide latitude to fill in the blanks with new rules and regulations. The law itself was 2,500 pages and the bureaucrats added another 17,500 pages of regulation. There are now seven pages of rules for every page of law. It is easy to see how the bureaucrats can take any law and bend it and expand it in any way they like. It is the bureaucrats whom decided which medications are approved and which are not; which hospitals are approved and which are not; which medical tests are approved and which are not; which medical procedures are approved and which are not; which doctor will be approved to attend to you and which ones you will not be able to see. Do you now understand the kind of power these bureaucrats have over all of our lives? These unelected,

76

unaccountable, unnamed bureaucrats are the real power in Washington D.C. and we have no authority over them. Congress likes to paint with a broad brush and leave the details to the bureaucrats but for the sake of our U.S. Citizen, for the sake of our society and our way of life, we must demand that Congress becomes intimately involved in each and every rule and regulation. Period!

I propose that Congress gain and maintain all final approval authority over each and every rule and regulation proposed by these bureaucrats. This authority is to be taken by the House of Representatives; the People's House. These proposed rules do not need to be voted on by the entire House, but rather the work can be divided between existing committees as determined by their area of authority, which will also depend upon which department within the Executive Branch department is proposing the rule.

These committee meetings are to be open to the public. The bureaucrats that are recommending the regulation will need to testify and present their case for passage. In addition, individual citizens and companies affected by the rule should be encouraged to testify before these committees; their support and/or objections are to be considered before any regulation is voted upon. Yes, this will slow down the process but that is a very, very good thing. We were a government of the people. Today we are a government of the bureaucrat. This will correct that, as it will constrain and limit their power. It will also put a name and face on each of these bureaucrats. I should think that a lot of us would like to know who is responsible for telling a cancer patient that their life saving medication will no longer be included in their health insurance plan.

There also needs to be a parallel open comment period during which ordinary citizens are also encouraged to comment on the recommended regulation. Passage of the proposed rule will require a simple majority vote from these House committees. This places authority and accountability where it belongs, with our elected officials. When each rule is approved, it must be listed in detail on a new and comprehensive website within 24 hours of passing.

If the U.S. Citizens do not like the job that the House is doing in this regard, it will soon become apparent in the next election; a nice Constitutional way to keep these rules and regulations in check.

Part Two
Term Limits Not Lifetime Employment

I propose that all bureaucrats whom are in any manner connected to the proposal of new rules and regulations be subject to term limits. These individuals are far too powerful and unaccountable. Their time in office must be limited. I recommend a term limit of four years. The term is to start at the beginning of the off year election, that is, the beginning of the third year of a Presidential term and ends at the end of the fourth year with a maximum of one term only per individual. All of these fore mentioned bureaucrats must be nominated by the President and then their appointment must be approved by the U.S. Senate.

I think we have been worried about term limits on the wrong people. Our politicians are subject to the vote of our U.S. Citizens; these bureaucrats are not. That must change if we are to remain a democratic republic. At present, these bureaucrats are ruling as they did during King George III's time.

It is this government within a government that we need to worry about! It is the bureaucrats' time in office that we need to control.

There is no downside to this idea from the U.S. Citizens point-of-view. It crosses the isle, includes all races, all nationalities and it does not attack or alienate anyone outside of government.

This will appeal to the Independents, the rank and file Democrats, the rank and file Republicans and I should hope, the Libertarians.

As with every other proposal, this one is focused on improving the lives of our U.S. Citizens along with safeguarding their places of employment and therefore, their jobs.

CHAPTER 11
How Big Is Too Big?

Too big is when it hurts more than it helps! Today, our government is a colossus with its nose in every aspect of our lives; and like all colossuses it requires a great deal of food, or in this case money. But our government's appetite for our money is never ending; enough will never be enough! Every year it requires more money than it takes in, so it borrows and borrows from a cast of countries, many of which are not our friends; and let's not forget that our own Federal Reserve is also one of our biggest creditors. How does that work? I mean, how can we be buying our own debt? Sounds like an oxymoron to me. But, unfortunately it is not!

Like all things that are out of control, this colossus will start to smash things. First, it has severely limited our freedoms and liberties and soon it will cripple our financial well being and eventually lead to a financial catastrophe. At present, we have over $18 Trillion in debt but what very few people are telling you is we also have additional unfunded obligations that are over $100 Trillion. That is a total obligation of over $118 Trillion! That is more than the total net worth of the USA which is around $85 Trillion. This total liability includes state and federal worker retirement programs along with other obligations like Social Security, Medicare, Medicaid and of course ObamaCare. A free society cannot live side by side with an oversized, overbearing government that is financially insolvent. The two are diametrically opposed to one another; only one will remain. It will be up to us which one goes and which one grows. I want more freedom and more liberty so I vote for a free society! Being free is our birthright, but as I have written, that right is being constrained by an ever increasing and intrusive big government, and big debt is one of the most severe constraints imaginable on a free people. Oversized organizations will never admit to being oversized, nor will they recognize it when it is obvious to everyone else. I recommend that we put this unwieldy beast on a diet!

I think it is ironic that we have a First Lady, who is leading a crusade to get our children to lose weight and exercise more. She is worried that their health will be poor when they are adults and that they will be placing a significant burden on our healthcare system, as well as having a negative impact on healthcare costs. The ironic part is she does not feel the same about the overweight and bloated government that her husband is building.

In fact, he is the all time heavy weight champ of a big, fat government, but to be fair, Bush 2 was a big spender as well, but even he is not in the same league as Obama. Like the First Lady, I am also concerned that fat is a heavy burden on us and it is having a very negative impact upon our individual lives and the lives of our children. I am glad that we both agree that fat is bad and thin is in! Of course, I am referring to a fat government! Big government brings a lot of pain to all of us. It intrudes into every aspect of our lives and is never, ever satisfied with enough. The bureaucrats will continue to think of new ways to run our lives, when all we want to do is live our lives. The remedy is a diet; a steady and consistent diet is the cure for our ills. The politicians do not get it. They just passed a cromnibus spending bill of over one trillion dollars. We are going broke and Congress and the SuperCitizens are having a spending party! There seems to be little difference between the DemoParty and the Establishment Republicans. It is time for a change!

The Conservative Solution
Plank Five
Zero Is The Place To Start

I propose that all government departments create a zero based budget. **That is, they must go back to zero and build their budgets from the ground up**. They will be required to justify each and every expense item, line-by-line, with the appropriate department head. The various department heads must in turn justify their departmental budgets with their superiors.

There is to be one overriding rule that is to be used to justify every expense line; all budgeted items must reflect a need versus a want. For instance, the State Department recently placed an order for liquor in the hundreds of thousands of dollars not because they needed the booze; rather it was the end of the budget year and they feared that not spending it meant it would not be there in the next budget, so they spent it. That is a perfect example of the difference between a need and a want. To put it bluntly, a need is an expenditure that is compelled by a separate law; a want is something that you may want to have but is not required by the rule of law. That is, it cannot be an earmarked item added to a fiscal budget or any other bill. That simple measure will be the new government mantra! It will be the yard stick that must be used to put this beast on a diet.

84

It may sound simple, but it is not as easy as it may seem, as many in government will not want to reduce any spending. The biggest impediment this procedure will face is the bureaucratic mindset in Washington; spend it or lose it. Such thinking must be challenged at every level in this type of budgeting process. Another equally weighted impediment will be the special spending programs for campaign contributors. These special interest paybacks are costing us big dollars and are a huge waste of our money. You see, our politicians look at our tax money as free money for them to use to repay their financial supporters. A prime example is the Travel Promotion Act that was set to expire in 2015. It is nothing more than a taxpayer funded PR campaign for Harry Reid's campaign contributors. The one trillion, one hundred billion 2014 cromnibus spending bill extended the funding for this TPA Billion Dollar program for another five years until 2020. And this is only one of a hundred special spending programs that filled this bloated trillion dollar cromnibus spending bill. (It is sad to see that it is business as usual in Washington D.C. and so soon after the 2014 elections but as I have written, they will keep spending and spending until we have a Conservative in the White House. I am hopeful that 2016 can be a transitional year for all of us.)

In conjunction with the zero based budget work being performed in D.C., a field audit must be conducted. The audit will require that all recipients of Disability Social Security, Medicare, Medicaid and Social Security Retirement be contacted and verified as accurate. In addition, a sizeable bounty will be announced and paid to anyone who reports verifiable fraudulent cases to the auditors. We must inspect what we expect! We need to better control fraud and waste. By the way, I am willing to bet that this audit will cost less than the TPA program that was named in the above paragraph.

The Executive Branch will need to make this zero based budgeting process as transparent as possible. They will also need to make it apparent to the American Public that our government can live within its means. When it comes to spending tax dollars, the government must be accountable to the U.S. Citizens. Only a freedom loving President will initiate this process, as he/she will recognize that excessive taxes are a significant constraint upon our economic freedom. How free can the U.S. Citizens be if they are working six to seven months for the government? When you add up all the local and federal taxes we pay, you can easily see that we are working more for the government than we are for our families and for ourselves. If nothing is done to reverse this runaway spending, then our children will be working nine to ten months for the government. We must give them a better future!

How can our current politicians possibly think that keeping us in economic servitude to the government is what our founding fathers had in mind when they created our form of government? How did we allow this to happen? How can we allow it to continue?

Sadly, neither moderate Republicans nor any insider from the DemoParty will ever endorse this type of budgeting process. They will never want to right this wrong. Money is power and they love both!

We need a Conservative President who will lift our U.S. Citizens out of servitude to our government.

At the end of this process, the finalized budget must be presented in part and in whole to the House of Representatives. Only the House can initiate spending programs and therefore, they are the starting point for approval of this work. In this way, the House's power is strengthened versus the Executive Branch as the various departments within the Executive Branch must justify their budgets line-by-line to the House for approval. Money is king in Washington D.C. and the House has the power of the purse. Like no other time in our history, it is most urgent for them to control the runaway spending of this government.

Once this process is initiated, the people will have more than a little to say about how this money should be spent or better yet, not spent.

Again, I do not see any downside to this proposal for the U.S. Citizen. Yes, I realize that there will be a lot of angst and hair pulling from those whose pet government program may be cut but we must learn to live within our tax revenue limits. The alternative will end in disaster for the USA and for the world.

It is my hope that all freedom loving individuals will embrace this one. An ever escalating debt is like a ball and chain around the ankles of all future generations. How can we continue to burden them? Don't we need to offer them the same bright futures that our parents offered to us?

CHAPTER 12
Poor Health Insurance Versus a Healthier Life

The DemoParty has challenged the Republican Party to come up with a socialized healthcare program better than ObamaCare. Let's look at what the DemoParty has offered: minimal health insurance for the poor through an expanded Medicaid program serviced by fewer and fewer doctors. In addition, they are looking to further increase the Medicaid roles by allowing non U.S. Citizens to sign up while looking the other way when it comes to deportation. They have mandated that everyone must have an approved health insurance policy or they will impose a tax on those who do not buy one. They are limiting the payouts of these policies and they are increasing the amount of money that the subscriber must pay, both for the policy itself, as well as increasing the deductible, once the subscriber uses the policy. It is nice to have the DemoParty in power; they tax you when you don't comply and when you do comply, they make you pay even more for less coverage. When do we benefit from their big wonderful program? The answer is never!

Their ObamaCare slogan should be "with more, you get less". More tax dollars spent for longer lines in the waiting room and less time with the doctor and even fewer doctors in the years to come. All the while, the poor were receiving health care at no cost to themselves in emergency rooms nationwide. How has their lot in life improved? They had better healthcare with less wait time before ObamaCare. And let's not forget about the state sponsored Medicaid programs costs. The Federal Government is picking up the added cost for the first three years, but after that the old formulas will apply and the states that agreed to expand their programs will be looking to their citizens for additional taxes. A lot to look forward to for the U.S. Citizens of those states!

For those earning up to 4 times the poverty line, a premium subsidy is available, but only for those who sign up on the government websites. In addition, the subsidy amount descends in value the closer your earnings are to the maximum level. But if you accept the subsidies up front and if your income should increase above the stated amount that you declared at the beginning of the program, then the IRS can demand that you repay some, if not all of the subsidies.

It is important to note that the subsidies are only available to those who buy their insurance directly through the federal government website or the state sponsored websites. That is, if you buy your insurance directly from the insurance provider, you will not qualify for any subsidies. Of course only the approved DemoParty insurance policies are available for the subsidies. And the lucky taxpayer is on the hook for all this spending.

The DemoParty has even made things more complicated. In their effort to make all states create and maintain an ObamaCare website, they wrote into law that subsidies will only be available through the state run websites. Well, more states chose not to build their own websites than those who did, so the Executive Branch stepped in and said that the subsidies will be available through the federal website as well. It turns out that this does not follow the very plain language of the law regarding subsidies and now it is being challenged in court. Several courts came down on both sides of this issue so the Supreme Court has again agreed to rule on ObamaCare regarding these subsidies. What a mess!

For those who do not qualify for the subsidies, all policies will carry a higher personal premium along with higher deductibles than their pre-ObamaCare policies. These policies will also feature a more limited list of approved medications under the prescription portion of the program. In addition, only a limited number of physicians and healthcare centers are eligible for payment under these insurance policies. Only the DemoParty decides what is covered, what doctors are available and what medications are available to the subscriber. And let us not forget that the DemoParty also created dozens of new panels that were established to do one thing, control costs and therefore control the U.S. Citizen.

They demanded that a healthy single male or a post-menopausal woman must buy insurance coverage for pregnancy and various other female medical needs even though they will never use these services. It is like demanding that an automobile driver must buy RV insurance and motorcycle insurance even if they do not own either one. The

91

DemoParty is at its best when they require you to buy things that are not in your own financial interest! What power!

Only the DemoParty will determine how much your premiums will be and how much of the bills you will pay out of pocket. They claim it is the industry's fault, but in truth it is their rules that determine what plans the insurance companies can profitably offer you. You have to give credit to the DemoParty, they know how to constrain you and make you compliant! Then, they claim that their hands are clean!

The DemoParty lied to us in order to pass this law and they continue to lie to us about the negative effects of their ObamaCare program; all the while they are looking us directly in our eyes. They are a bold lot!

What does it matter that there are fewer doctors servicing more patients? I liken it to buttering a loaf of bread with only two pats of butter; each slice will receive a few molecules of butter, but it will be so thin you will neither see it nor taste it. It doesn't matter to the DemoParty; they still claim that they are helping the economically disadvantaged. The problem is that there are still millions without insurance coverage.

Of course, they are causing people to lose employer sponsored healthcare coverage, while at the same time, causing many more to lose their individual policies that do not meet their new standards. This is the first case I can think of where the majority of people are forced to financially sacrifice for the social benefit of the few. No, I am wrong. The English Monarchs did the same in reverse; they bled the peasants of

92

their money, their freedom and their liberty for the benefit of a few noblemen and their families. The DemoParty is doing the same thing but they just turned the table around. It seems that we are just in a different flavored soup from our colonial forefathers; but the temperature is still boiling hot!

So, the DemoParty has cooked up something that they call healthcare when it is something else entirely. It is not healthcare at all but health insurance and a very low quality one at that. It is terrifically expensive and compulsory; so they love it! It has done little to improve the poor's access to healthcare, but that is beside the point. It has done and will do a great deal of damage to the healthcare industry in total, so as the industry crumbles; the DemoParty is hoping that they can force a single payer program upon an unsuspecting U.S. Citizen. That sounds familiar doesn't it? By the way, some are claiming that this program is really a redistribution program; yes, it is, but that is what the DemoParty does best. So, why is anyone surprised?

I think that this program demonstrates the difference between the two parties as well as anything else. The Republicans are all in for business and the wealthy. They claim to be concerned about the middle class but I think it is primarily the white collar middle class, not the blue collar middle class. They are focused on protecting the wealthy and developing new advantages for the advantaged.

The DemoParty is all in for socialism. They want to control the playing field by controlling the healthcare industry

93

and forcing the U. S. Citizens to have insurance policies. They are not interested in being a fair minded referee but rather the boss and implementer of programs that they deem fair to all. Of course, this often has the opposite effect but that makes no difference to them. They are intent on taking from the Republican supporters and they see themselves as the only ones intellectually able to properly divide the spoils of their tax upon tax policies; this they see as their mission.

We are caught in the crossfire and no one from either warring camp has our best interests in mind. Neither political party is concerned about enhancing our lives, our freedoms or our way of life. Neither is vigilantly safeguarding our freedoms or our liberties. One or the other or both will gladly throw us under the bus if it means they will win the support of their special interest groups. I do not know about you, but I do not look good with tire tread marks all over my body!

Back to Healthcare; the DemoParty has challenged the Republicans to come up with their own version of a healthcare bill; a challenge that the Republicans are loath to reply. But if it is truly healthcare that we are concerned about then let's get to it.

I want the U.S. Citizen to live a healthy, active, longer, pain-free life. Healthcare is all about quality, affordability and access.

The Conservative Solution
Plank Six
A Six Part Proposal
Part One
More Butter Please!

Each year about 18,000 medical students become doctors in the U.S. The total number of medical doctors in the country is a little over 800,000. That is a replacement rate of about 2.3% which does little to improve the ratio of doctors to patients, especially taking into account all the baby boomers that are reaching retirement age.

I propose that we offer to pay all tuition, housing, clothing and transportation expenses for up to 40,000 medical students each year beginning in 2017. Of course the number of students receiving these grants will depend upon the ability to field a qualified pool of students. The program will have a five year life and will terminate at the end of the five year period. All expenses will be paid for every student in the program until their graduation from Medical School. Each student is expected to complete their studies within a reasonable and acceptable time frame; exceptions will be granted for justifiable reasons.

This is not a student loan program but rather a tax free grant to the student from the U.S. Citizens. We need more doctors and this is an efficient way to produce more of them.

There will be qualifiers, as each student must first be accepted by an accredited medical school before applying for this grant. Second, there are strings attached and they are meaningful both to the student as well as to us, the U.S. Citizen. A contractual agreement will be entered into between the student and the government.

The American Medical Association will play a key role in this program as they will fill the role of advisor and in some cases they will also play the role of arbiter. The AMA will determine which study of medicine the student will follow. This will be written into the student's contract. Some will become surgeons; others will study internal medicine and so on. The AMA will make that determination based upon the student's individual abilities and career desires as well as the medical needs of the U.S. Citizen. The goal of the program is to make more doctors available, without lowering medical standards.

This will be a voluntary program. Any student wishing to pursue their own medical career will not be eligible for the grant. Student loans will remain available along with scholarships as they are today; there is no wish to interrupt anyone's dreams of following a specific field of medicine.

Any unexpected consequences, like skyrocketing tuition, are to be avoided. Any medical school participating in this program will need to agree to keep non program students' tuition within the range of increases of the five preceding years. That is, if tuition costs have increased an averaged 4%

over the five previous years, then it will follow that future increases will be in line with the previous five years. In short, it would be unacceptable for government tuition payments to unjustly increase the tuition costs of a medical school. (My concern stems from the way in which Medicare payments have spurred increased medical expenses.)

In addition to the field of study, the student's contract will detail the geographic location where the student will practice medicine. I think it only fair for each enrollee to be aware of his/her assigned location before they sign any contract. It could be a major metropolitan location or a small town in a large geographical state. Again, it would depend upon the need and the AMA should be the final judge.

In some ways, this group of students will be the next generation of indentured servants. And like the indentured servants of old, they will have a ten year time frame within which they will provide their services to the U.S. Citizen at the market rate. During this time, they must remain within their field and within the area assigned to them by the AMA. There is no free lunch!

There will also be similar programs for nurse practitioners and lab technicians.

Hopefully, we will see an increase in the number of qualified medical doctors, nurses and lab technicians. It may be that the program will need to be longer than the five year period that I suggested, but I would think that if there is a need, the program would be extended.

97

Finally, we need to listen to the AMA regarding reimbursement rates to doctors. Our doctors are not a cost item to be controlled; they deserve our respect and our appreciation and should be reimbursed accordingly.

Part Two
How To Pay For These Grants

The USA is the proud owner of thousands of large vacant federal buildings throughout the country. They are being managed by the General Services Administration (GSA). There are over 76,000 empty or partially used buildings that cost the U.S. Taxpayers over 1.6 Billion Dollars just to manage each year. These numbers are according to the Office of Management and Budget (OMB).

I propose that all of these buildings be sold either individually or sold in bundles. Either way, the selling process is to be open, honest and controlled by the OMB. There must not be any political favors involved in the sale of these buildings. We do not need a repeat of Senator Dianne Feinstein's husband's involvement with the sale of some of our Post Office buildings. His real estate company may earn over 1 Billion Dollars on these transactions. No relatives, no friends, no campaign contributors and no hint of any type of favoritism should arise from the sale of these excess federal buildings.

The revenue generated from the sale of these buildings as well as the $1.6 billion annual expense is to be used to fund the above grant program as well as to buy or build new, smaller outpatient medical facilities throughout the U.S. These are to be located near hospitals in major metropolitan areas and regional health care hospitals in rural areas. They are to be licensed and regulated by the state and local municipalities as they are today. They will be run as a non- profit entity and will receive some funding from the federal government. In short, they will be run in a similar manner as National Public Radio and the Public Broadcasting System stations are today. They will conduct fundraising campaigns four times a year over the NPR and PBS stations. All donations will be tax deductible, as they are for NPR/PBS donations. All monetary donations will go to the local outpatient facilities to cover operating costs. The federal and state governments will make up any shortfalls. The buildings will be given to the state and subject to state regulations and licensing.

These facilities will be opened on a preplanned schedule and they will be setup to perform minor surgeries, routine lab work, outpatient service, sick visits and routine wellness visits. These facilities will be staffed by the above doctors, nurse practitioners and lab technicians whom participate in the programs as described in the proceeding section.

Part Three
Equipping Facilities

Equipping these outpatient facilities will again follow a non-profit set of guidelines. Just as the PBS TV stations have equipped their studios and offices, the same methods will be followed in order to equip these outpatient facilities. In addition, manufacturers of medical equipment will be able to donate their products and be granted tax deductions equal to 150% of the actual production cost of the equipment. The same will be true for day-to-day supplies like bandages, gloves, cotton, paper, computers, and so forth. The manufacturers that donate these supplies will receive the same 150% tax deduction.

Obviously, there will be a need to purchase some equipment which will be paid by the federal government.

Part Four
The Patient and Intervention

These outpatient facilities will be open to all U.S. Citizens and any foreign citizen as long as they produce proof that they are in our country legally. All health insurance programs will be accepted and for those who are uninsured, the costs will be divided between the state and the federal government. The foreign citizen will be treated as long as their insurance is verified and qualified. More serious cases will be referred to a nearby hospital and if the case is life threatening then the patient will quickly be admitted and the payment will be appropriately handled.

Substance abuse diagnosis will play a prominent role at these facilities. Any patient displaying these symptoms will be referred to an intervention facility and will be required to fully participate in these programs. Upon a second visit, if the patient has not participated in a substance intervention program, then they will either agree to be immediately enrolled in such a program or they will no longer be treated at these outpatient facilities. It is a blunt and seemingly harsh directive to force any individual to participate in an intervention program, but the U.S. Citizen should never be placed in the position of an enabler to substance abuse. Unfortunately, intervention is the only answer for these individuals and a healthier, active, longer life for all our U.S. Citizens is our stated goal.

Part Five
The Mission

The mission of these facilities is to help the patient lead longer, healthier and more active lives.

This program would need to be tested in a few limited locations and if successful and if affordable, it can gradually be rolled out nationwide.

Mandated health insurance will cease to exist in the U.S.; our U.S. Citizens will be free to choose any insurance policy from any company nationwide. The insurance industry will still be regulated by the state in which the insurance company is headquartered. This will lower the premiums for those who can afford to buy insurance. (The enhancing elements from ObamaCare, like allowing coverage for pre-existing diseases, will remain a part of all policies.) In addition, any company large or small that was offering health insurance to their employees and their retirees will once again need to offer these same policies to all. It is not the role of the government to take on cost expenses that once belonged to businesses.

Again, those U.S. Citizens who cannot afford insurance will be allowed free access to these outpatient facilities as they become available. There are still many U.S. Citizens in our country who are not eligible for Medicare and these facilities would provide them access to quality healthcare.

Part Six
Not The Moon And The Stars

We were given a mission in the early sixties by President Kennedy; land a man on the moon. Today, the NASA program is a shell of its former self, running limited programs. I guess you could say that Homeland Security is absorbing some of these budget dollars, but NASA was reaching for the stars, while Homeland Security is reaching into our personal lives, a place they do not belong.

I propose that we initiate another daring project with the exception that this one be Earthbound.

We must set a target of ten years to find a cure for cancer. I know that this is a very difficult and varied disease, but we as a nation must put our resources behind such a project. There have been and will be no easy answers, but if it was easy then we would not need such a program. In the 1960's, we pulled together all the scientists that made the NASA program a success; we can do it again with the men and women of medical research science. We must find a cure or continue to succumb to this disease. I vote for a cure!

There will be no false hopes built on this program nor should there be any political speeches about what a great program this is or any other grand pronouncements. It will entail years of hard work and significant expenditures of treasure, but this disease in all its forms must be met and conquered with all our country's might and power. This is our gift to the U.S. Citizen, a healthier life. We must win this fight and we will win it; if we make the commitment that I am proposing.

After all, the role of government is not to micro manage your life or your business or to interfere with your freedoms or your pursuit of happiness. Its role is to focus on creating an environment where anyone can prosper and realize their dreams; and a cure for cancer plays a significant role in this environment.

Healthcare Summary

More doctors not less; more medical facilities closer to patients not empty buildings with wasteful maintenance spending; more medical staff not less; free healthcare through Medicaid for those who cannot afford it; lower premiums with more choices for those who can afford it; free healthcare for those who do not qualify for Medicaid and finally, God willing, a real cure for cancer.

What I am recommending is better access to affordable, high quality healthcare not insufficient health insurance and limited prescription availability. This program meets this goal and provides our U.S Citizens with more freedom of choice; freedom to choose your own doctors, your own prescription plan, and your own hospital. Best of all, it uses tax dollars that are wasted on empty buildings and puts those dollars to work for the U.S. Citizen.

CHAPTER 13

To Have Or Not To Have?
Whether 'Tis Nobler For The Fed To Make The Rich Richer Or The Middle Class Poorer?

Ah, the Federal Reserve! We salute you! You are the enlightened protector of our fragile economy, you are the gods who walk among us lesser beings, you are the true gifts to mankind (not to mention your gifts to the rich). You are the chosen ones who bring dead banks back to life. It is you who smoothed the troubled automobile waters by allowing sub-prime borrowers to once again receive automobile loans through companies like Blackrock's Exeter Finance (and then they bundle them into securities and sell them...just like the mortgage meltdown). It is you who move markets with a key stroke and yes, it is you who ended that nasty free stock market.

We whose income is shrinking against a backdrop of higher and higher prices; we who are about to slip below the poverty line; we who make do with less; we salute you! For you are the super beings who brought us excess liquidity and a permanent zero interest rate to soften the economic blow after we moved our manufacturing overseas. You who gave us the dot-com bubble, the housing bubble, and now you are dazzling us with the zenith of all your works, the greatest of illusions; a stock market bubble. The miracle of your zero interest rates are compelling companies to borrow more and more money with which they can buy back more and more of their stock and fire more and more of their employees. Your marvels have lifted the yoke off of senior business executives and shown them that they no longer need to build their business, they no longer need concern themselves about earning incremental revenue, they just pass your magic disappearing fairy dust across their income statements and buy back their own shares. Poof! Their profits per share rise and everyone is rich. What difference does it make that our companies no longer build anything? We owe it all to the world of central planning!

What difference does it make that retires who worked hard and saved their money are getting near zero return on their money? Who among you should care that you have turned their golden years to lead? Why bother with such trivia!

We should all just relax and just let our money ride on the Federal Reserve Roulette Wheel; who cares if all the chips fly off the board every few years? Besides, the Federal Reserve was created by bankers for bankers and has always been owned by the world's richest families. What difference does it make that the Federal Reserve is not part of our federal government? (I have become very fond of the statement; "What difference does it make?" ...thank you Madam Secretary!) After all, it has been authorized by Congress to control the management of the U.S. Dollar, the overnight interest rates and the regulation of our banking business.

The Fed has played a pivotal role for the banks. Who else is going to shift all of the bad assets from the banks onto the Fed's balance sheet and then on to the U.S. Treasury and then to the U.S. Citizen? Who else will continue the constant bank funding process so that they may show a profit? All of this will end in a tragedy for the U.S. Citizens, but who cares?

Of course, this money is not for lending to small business or to be lent to individuals (except auto loans), rather it is for the banks to invest so they can prop-up their financial results. By the way, if you do not know, banks are very reluctant to lend money when annual GDP is growing at 4.5% or lower.

The Fed's continuous expansion of our money supply has also been a great help to all of those companies that sell products and services to the rich; like Tiffany's, Mercedes Benz and a few yacht companies. Just check out the price increases of vintage and rare sports cars, their prices are up 1000%. The rich love the Federal Reserve!

It's not the Fed's fault that Wal-Mart's and Dollar General's shoppers are not doing so well. It's those stupid middle class folks who are just paying too much for ObamaCare, diesel fuel, and food. It's their fault!

What's even more alarming, for the first time in our history; the Fed is a major purchaser of our own debt. You may ask, how can any country build a strong economy when they are buying their own debt? I simply do not know. But, I

110

can tell you that I have a friend that tried this once. He applied for more and more credit cards and then shifted his debt from existing cards to new cards. His wallet was three inches thick! No joke! It ended badly.

But, the Fed's bond buying doesn't cause any concern for the DemoParty; they love it; they can spend, spend, spend and the Fed buys, buys, buys. I wonder who has responsibility for cleaning this one up. Oh, that's right, it's not the rich, not big business, not big banks; it's the U.S. Citizen. How marvelous!

Regarding all those assets (mortgages) that the Fed is buying from the banks; what is the Fed doing with them? Are they passing them on to the U.S. Treasury or some other entity or are they just keeping them on their own books? And speaking of the books, where are all those bad derivatives that the banks were holding back in 2008? Did they just blow away? Where are they and how many trillions had they lost in 2008? Worse yet, who owns them today and what are they worth today? Don't tell me; we own them! Even worse, the top five U.S. Banks are now holding more than Two Hundred Trillion Dollars in new derivatives; that is not a "B" as in billion but a "T" as in Trillion! Boom, Boom, Bust!

Another question if you please, since you and Treasury forced through the FASB rule change from mark-to-market asset valuations to mark-to-model valuations, the banks can place any value they want on any of their bad mortgages. What? The banks self-determine the current value of the mortgages they own? But the homes that secured the

111

mortgages are still worth less than the mortgage. What is stopping the banks from expanding this to every other asset they own or ever will own? What about all those fresh new securities that are backed by sub-prime car loans? Will the banks be able to use the same revised FASB asset valuation rule? That is, will the automobiles be valued as new cars on a permanent basis? It makes one wonder!

Excuse me. I need to ask one more question. In all your bank stress tests did you include in the various scenarios a rise in the overnight interest rate? What happens if interest rates go all the way to 1% or, heaven forbid, 5%.? At what interest rate will the banks fail? I think we need to know. I also think that hell will freeze over before we ever see a 1% overnight interest rate. That's how bad I think things are with most of our big banks! I hope I am wrong.

In this bazaar world created by the Federal Reserve our stock market has become totally detached from reality. The worse our economy gets, the higher the stock market goes because the investors think that the Fed will continue to keep interest rates at zero and maybe even begin a new QE 4 program. Wouldn't that be nice?

Janet Yellen, through all the pomp and ceremony and the fawning, attentive financial press hanging on your every word and participle, you are in reality only the handmaiden of the very wealthy and powerful whose bidding you perform.

You and your cohorts are the third main cause of our ever increasing wealth/income gap.

What will give your conscience solace after all is said and done and we the U.S. Citizen, who have received little benefit from your QE programs and zero interest rate, must yet again endure the pain of another bubble busting? Will you be busy planning your next imaginary economy?

There is no better example of your destructive handy work than Kimberly-Clark. This company makes such familiar brands as Kleenex, Huggies, Kotex and Depend. They make great products and are a great company but they, like every other company that is listed on the NYSE, need to show an increased profit on a per share basis. So, they announced a share repurchase program for up to 40 million shares. They also announced a dividend of $.84 per share. They announced they are spinning off their Health Care Division. And finally, they announced a restructuring program that is aimed at reducing costs by eliminating 1,300 jobs. All of these actions have increased the value of their stock. You see the more our economy is destroyed, the higher the stock market goes up.

I have chosen Kimberly-Clark because they are performing the four main actions that many companies are performing today.

1) They are using their cash flow along with the Fed's low interest rate to buy back up to Five Billion Dollars of their own stock. They, like most other companies today, view this expenditure as having more value than investing in their business.

2) They are spinning off a key division to maximize their

113

stock value. This will also allow the new company to initiate their own cost cutting and stock buyback programs.

3) They are passing on their excess cash to the stock holders in the form of dividends.

4) They are firing 1,300 people.

Cutting through all the false claims of a growing economy by pointing to a climbing stock market, Kimberly-Clark's real world actions lift the Fed's veil and show us the destruction their actions are having upon our economy. Kimberly-Clark is not investing in their business. None of their actions will improve our economy. They are increasing the ranks of the unemployed as senior management is forced to cut costs because our economy is not growing. Clearly, the Federal Reserve's actions are hurting the U.S. Citizen.

Like us, Kimberly-Clark is a victim of the economy. All of these actions are the result of the Federal Reserve's zero interest rate policy and their QE programs. Their central planning is killing our job market and preventing any real investment from taking place in our country. Investments that create wealth, investments that build a stronger middle class, and make for a stronger USA are taking a backseat because these companies know there is no real forecasted growth in the USA.

Here are a few more recent job cut announcements:
• Microsoft announced their biggest ever job cut to take

114

effect in 2015 of 18,000 employees.

- Dow Chemical, our largest chemical company cut 2,400 jobs and closed 20 manufacturing plants in 2012.
- Caterpillar cut over 13,000 jobs the last two years.
- American Express announced a 5,400 job cut in 2013.
- Verizon announced a 1,000 job cut in November 2014.
- Sprint announced a cut of 2,000 jobs in November 2014.
- Boeing announced a cut of 2,000 jobs in September 2014.
- Coca-Cola announced it will be cutting jobs in 2015, but would not give a number. It wants to cut costs by three billion dollars, so the job cuts will be significant. A lot to look forward to for those employees.
- Merck Co. Announced 16,000 job cuts in late 2013.
- Intel announced 5,000 job cuts in 2014.
- Hewlett-Packard has announced job cuts of over 100,000 in the past two years.
- In 2015, IBM announced it will be planning to lay off 26% of their employees which may be well over 100,000 people.

There are many, many, many more job cuts that have been announced during the last few years. All of these cuts are being done to drive up the stock price of all these companies and once again it makes my point; the better the stock market does, the worse our economy is performing.

The Federal Reserve is obsessed with the stock market because it is the only thing they can point to and say that our economy is improving; but in reality the higher the market rises, the worse our economy is doing. And I do not see an end to the Federal Reserve's interference in our economy. The stock market is obsessed with the Fed's low interest rates as margin accounts and stock repurchase programs are dependent upon the low interest rates. And let us not forget our federal government is also dependent upon the Fed's low interest rate. You need to keep in mind that over 270 Billion of our tax revenue is spent on servicing our national debt and that is at today's extremely low interest rates. If the interest rate climbs only fractionally, it would be a disaster for our federal budget. We simply could not afford it. The result is that the Fed has created this list of dependents and they will never be able to raise interest rates above one percent. This points out how weak our economy is as a result of their interference and there is no way out for them that does not spell disaster for us.

The Conservative Solution
Plank Seven
We need a Séance

I propose that Janet Yellen be our spiritualist and conduct a séance with the House members of the Committee on Financial Services. She can attempt to communicate with the spirits of all the former Federal Reserve Chairmen and explain to the committee members what actions the Fed has taken in the last two decades since the great migration of jobs to China.

As well, she can open the book of spells that the Federal Reserve calls its accounting books for their examination and have an outside audit performed in order to lift the Fed's veil of secrecy and extinguish this demon from the pocketbooks of the U.S. Citizen. They have never made an accounting to the people of this country. It is time they made it!

This is really no joking matter. The Federal Reserve is not the CIA nor is it the DOD; yet the details of their actions remain secret. Their impact on our day-to-day lives is no secret; they clearly have had a significant negative effect upon the U.S. Citizens. They blow bubble after bubble and wreck havoc upon us; yet there is never any explanation or apology for their greedy actions that favor themselves, their wealthy owners and their constituents. They were never given authority to be our central economic planner; they just took it

117

upon themselves with the blessings of the DemoParty. Congress never gave them the authority to buy our own debt, they did it anyway. **How can we have a privately owned company in charge of our economy? How can a free country remain free when our economy is run by a central planning organization that is not part of our government and is not accountable to the U.S. Citizen?** We need a return to the gold standard, which will reign in these bankers and limit their destructive money printing QE programs.

We need a Conservative President that will call the Federal Reserve to task and compel them to explain their actions to the U.S. Citizen.

This proposal should warm the hearts of rank and file Libertarians, Democrats and Republicans. It is a win for 90% of our U.S. Citizens!

Another word of warning! I think Obama will never allow the Federal Reserve to raise the overnight interest rate. I think Obama wants to walk away from office and leave a financial mess for the next President. I recommend that the Republican Congress do whatever they can to lift this veil of secrecy surrounding the Federal Reserve before the 2016 election and expose Obama's financial mess. Otherwise, it will be a ticking time bomb for what may be a Republican Presidency. Audit them now or suffer the consequences later!

CHAPTER 14

The Big, Big Boss And his Big Boss Empire

We voted for Hope and Change and we got Oppression and Autocracy. Mr. Obama is well on his way to becoming our first and hopefully our last autocrat. You may think that the term autocrat is too severe, so let's just call him The Big, Big Boss. Like a petulant child, when he does not like what Congress is doing and he does not like the U.S. Citizen voting down his agenda, he throws a fit and completely ignores Congress. This Boss of Bosses no longer feels he needs to uphold his sworn duty to faithfully execute our laws, he and he alone decides which laws he will execute and which he will ignore. Only he decides which millions of people he prosecutes and which millions he will not, all based on his very fuzzy defining criteria that separates the two groups. Like Harry Reid in the Senate, when a DemoParty member does not like the way things are heading, they do their best to write new rules or in this case, write new laws. The Big, Big Boss in the White House is now writing and passing his own laws for which he has no authority to make. His actions are more than a slap in the face of Congress; they are a slap in the face of the U.S. Citizen. When he ignores Congress he is ignoring the will of the people.

Our President of the United States has decided on his own to enhance the lives of the illegal aliens while at the same

119

time diminishing our lives. Who is he working for? It is most certainly not the U.S. Citizen.

His Big Boss attitude did not develop overnight. It started out very early in his first term, with the lies and misleading statements involving the passage of ObamaCare. When his actions were given the stamp of approval by the U.S. Supreme Court, he felt further empowered to take more and more unilateral actions and Harry Reid protected his flank by pocketing every objection voted on by the House. The DemoPress continued to ignore any bad news stories, so his confidence in his own power continued to grow. All the while, he was subverting the government bureaucrats toward his own political views. These government bureaucrats are his soldiers that make up his Big Boss Empire. Now these same bureaucrats are actively denigrating and increasingly controlling the lives and the livelihoods of our U.S. Citizens. They are finding more and more ways to compel us to behave in ways that are detrimental to our own financial well being.

These underlying, denigrating attitudes of the Big Boss are now flowing throughout his Empire and have replaced the old values of respect for our U.S. Citizens. Let's look at our current President's attitude toward the private U.S. Citizen versus his attitude toward the government employee. How he views these two groups is how all the bureaucrats within the Executive Branch will view themselves and us. Unfortunately, we are not doing so well with the current administration.

The President has made it very clear that he elevates the level of importance of a government employee to twice the level of the private workforce employee. This is well documented in his *Pay as You Earn Plan* regarding repayment of student loans. As long as you remain current on your loan repayment, a government employee will be forgiven the remaining balance of their federal loan at the end of 10 years (120 payments), but a private sector employee must wait 20 years (240 payments) before being forgiven any remaining debt. You see a government employee has twice the value of a private citizen. Do you get the picture? Even though you and I pay the salary of the government employee, you and I are considered to be the lower class. We fund the government, but we are looked down upon by our superiors in the federal government. This same attitude existed during King George III's rule over the colonies. We are the lesser citizen, the unwashed masses who are to be controlled and taxed. Do you think that the government bureaucrats are tuned in to his attitude? Do you think it plays a significant role when they are enforcing their overburdening regulations? Are they quick to level excessive penalties and even call in armed enforcement personnel? Is their attitude toward us one of superiority and control? The answer is quite simply 'Yes'.

How about an even more startling comparison? Let's compare the U.S. Citizen to the Citizens of the World. Again, we are not doing so well. The Executive Branch is dedicated to enhancing the lives of the foreign citizen who crosses our southern border illegally; they are not interested in enhancing our lives. They are also interested in enhancing the lives of the Chinese Citizen, the Hungarian Citizen and the Indonesian Citizen by creating jobs in their markets; they are not interested in enhancing our job market. In fact, each foreign citizen whose life is enhanced means that our lives are denigrated; more government spending, more taxes, fewer job opportunities and longer unemployment lines. Not leaving well enough alone, our President has now determined that the foreign citizen's right to obtain a U.S. Visa and travel to the U.S. is more important than our continued good health. That is, he is allowing those exposed to Ebola to enter our country and travel within our midst. Again, this Executive Branch is focused on enhancing the lives of the foreign citizen, not ours. We are the lesser citizen, even when compared to a foreign citizen. Last place again! First, he favors the government bureaucrat over us and now he favors the foreign citizen over us. What does that tell you?

Do you think that the above mentioned bureaucrat picks up on this attitude? They already feel that they are superior to the U.S. Citizen as previously described; now they also think that every foreign citizen is superior to us. Now, they think nothing about rushing the illegals into remote parts of our country, which is aiding them and harming us. Who do these bureaucrats really work for? It is not the U.S. Citizen.

So, this attitude of our President has spread throughout the Executive Branch. It is now an easy jump to understand

what happened within the IRS. If Obama doesn't like a
Supreme Court ruling, then his bureaucrats, who have long ago
picked up on 'If you want to keep your job get with the
program', are all too keen to thwart our individual freedoms as
provided by a Supreme Court ruling. Of course the DemoParty
has also thought of ways to ensure that lower level bureaucrats
share their enthusiasm for squelching our free speech. They
have strategically placed true believers into key management
positions throughout the various departments and it is they who
will ensure that directives are no longer questioned. That is
how we ended up with the current IRS/Tea Party scandal.
Imagine that! They are turning our own government against us.
Oh, and it is important to keep in mind that these same
bureaucrats will keep their jobs long after the President is out
of office.

Another example is the way in which the EPA is
expanding their reach into every aspect of our daily lives.
They are devising new rules that will obsolete our coal burning
power plants and passing the costs on to the users. Never mind
that we had nothing to do with the decision to use coal in the
first place. Never mind that our tax dollars paid for the
construction of dams throughout our country. Those facilities
are EPA approved, so they get a pass while we who fall within
the coal plant areas will be punished and bled dry with
excessive penalties, while other citizens will avoid these new
taxes. So now, depending upon where you live, the federal
government will punish innocent citizens and reward others

just because of where they live. I thought we were one country and that we would all be treated equally. I guess the EPA sees it differently.

The EPA should tax all equally or tax none of us. If the federal government has a problem with coal burning plants, then the federal government should construct EPA approved electrical producing facilities at taxpayer expense for everyone, not just the select few.

Not satisfied with their level of control over our lives, the EPA is issuing new rules regarding all water on your land to include all forms of water: ponds, run-off, standing water and ground water and how it is to be treated. This will be their broadest expanse of their power ever! **Imagine what this will do to all of our farmers!** All of this they are doing without Congress, without the will of the people! They are truly the unelected government within the government.

There is still one more alarming area of concern in which these bureaucrats are planning to control us and make us comply. This administration is working within the United Nations Organization to sign a treaty covering stricter international global warming standards. They are attempting to do this without the approval of Congress. As you know, all treaties must be approved by the U.S. Senate. They are attempting to side step Congress and the Will of the People through an attempt to add this agreement as a clause to a previously approved treaty or by other more devious means. They are a slippery bunch!

One other comment regarding attitude; we have all been hearing commentary regarding the President's lack of attachment to his job. I think it goes much deeper. I do not think that this President has been or ever will be emotionally attached to the U.S. Citizen. I know he is emotional about race relation problems and the way the police conduct themselves in minority areas, but when the President gives a speech regarding the beheading of a U.S. Citizen by a terrorist and then immediately sallies forth to play a game of golf; I think there is more than a slight disconnect between our President and the U.S. Citizen. His actions were more than just being cool-headed or keeping his emotions in check. It lacked something basic to our nature, basic to being a U.S. Citizen. The idea that someone or some group thought that they could do this to us and then get away with it is counter to our very nature. We, more than any other country, care about one another and when we are attacked in such a manner it strikes us deep inside and generates a visceral reaction at the injustice and inhumane acts being performed by a terrorist group. It's a gut reaction. I did not see any of this in our President. It has caused me to think that this President is not just disenchanted with his office, but rather he is not emotionally attached to the U.S. Citizen. I think that this is true and it is more than a little tragic for all of us.

Add to this, his ability to look us straight in the eye and lie to us; not once, not twice, but multiple times. Add to this, his administration working behind the scenes on more and more intrusive ways to spy on us and control our lives. He is dead-set on making us comply with his personal rules and regulations. Add to this, his desire to grant amnesty to millions of illegal aliens who are here to supplant us in the workforce and drain our treasury. We deserve better!

Our individual state governments are being side-stepped or just plain ignored by these bureaucrats. Their rights are our rights and they are being trampled upon and pushed aside by this Executive Branch and its bureaucrats. Our freedom loving founding fathers wanted to keep power as close to the people as possible. They wanted to prevent a powerful federal government that ruled by edict. Unfortunately that is what we have today. My proposal enhances the states power and provides more control at the local level, which is our level, the U.S. Citizen. Keep in mind, that local control means a freer society.

So, if better days are ever to appear, we will need a Conservative in the White House to lead and a Republican majority in both Houses of Congress to solve this problem.

A solution needs to be found that will give an active and real-time voice to the U.S. Citizen; one that will reflect the approval or disapproval of the U.S. Citizen; one that provides them with an actionable presence in the bureaucrat's activities. What is needed is a solution that will allow our U.S. Citizens the ability to quickly let our federal bureaucrats know we are pleased or displeased with their actions.

126

If you are thinking that I am only concerned about the current administration, keep in mind that an overbearing, intrusive Executive Branch can come from the left or the right of the political spectrum. Remember Nixon? Correcting this problem is in our best interest, placing more power in the hands of the U.S. Citizen is most certainly in our interest and where it belongs. The problem is most bureaucrats act like they are our boss and that we work for them. It is time to remind them that the USA is a government By the People, For the People and not By the Bureaucrat, For the Special Interest. This plan is bold and it solves the problem in a unique way without interfering with the line of authority within the Executive Branch.

The Conservative Solution
Plank Eight
People Do What You Pay Them To Do

This has been a universal rule throughout our written history and it is one of the main drivers supporting Plank Eight. You and I do the work we are paid to do! And it holds true no matter the type of government running a country; it is true in Communist China, Germany, France, Spain, Indonesia, Iran and the United States. It does not matter if you work for a small company or a large international company. While the relationship between being paid well for your work and being paid poorly for your work is dependent upon your performance; the overall general rule remains a constant. If you do the work as assigned and you do it well, you will be paid well; if you do it poorly, you will be paid poorly or not at all, as in you are fired. But the rule itself is always true. Think about it in your own life, you perform the work that your boss wants you to perform and the same holds true for every other paid worker. But like all rules, there are exceptions. If you are an unpaid volunteer you still perform the assigned tasks but you are not paid, which is why they call it volunteering.

There is also one other important driver supporting Plank Eight; putting the U.S. Citizen between the politician and everything important in their lives. As I have explained, the

128

DemoParty wants to come between us and everything in our lives. **It is my counter strategy to place the U.S. Citizen between the politician and everything of importance to him or her.** In this case, I want to place the U.S. Citizen between the President and his bureaucrats; not in a way that hinders direct line of authority or their ability to work; but while it does not interfere with line authority, it does make the bureaucrat more accountable to the U.S. Citizen. Placing the U.S. Citizen in such a position will produce a better, more responsive, more respectful bureaucrat and will make the focus of their work not controlling us but rather enhancing the lives of our U.S. Citizens above all else. Sounds very good to me!

I recommend that a new Federal Department be created, called the Department of Citizen Service (DCS). This department will have two main responsibilities:

• **Their first responsibility** will be to provide to the U.S. Citizens a cumulative performance review of each department and agency within the Executive Branch, except the CIA and the Defense Department and parts of both Homeland Security and the DOJ.

There will be two separate appraisals generating two separate evaluations which, when completed, will be blended into one overall appraisal every six months. Part one will be an overall department performance review, including all agencies within each department. These appraisals will be the sole responsibility of the DCS citizen agents; the performance reviews will be completed and published every six months.

129

They will include an evaluation of all rules and regulations enacted during the previous six months, along with the various actions taken by the agency and the department. They will evaluate areas such as:

- Did they enhance the lives of our U.S. Citizens?
- Did they deteriorate the lifestyles of our U.S. Citizens? In what specific way?
- Did they help all Citizens or only a select few?
- Did they harm some Citizens and help other Citizens? In what specific way?
- Did they in any way help special interests groups?
- Did they help campaign contributors?
- Did they help only certain corporations?
- Did they punish only certain corporations?
- Did they encourage job development or harm it?
- Did they help the Foreign Citizen?
- Did they give more power to the United Nations and diminish self rule in the USA?
- Were steps taken to speed up a process as a favor to one specific individual or group?
- Were all investigations initiated on a timely basis and were they thoroughly completed?
- Was racial bias demonstrated through any specific actions?

Part two of the appraisal process will be executed by the individual U.S. Citizen and U.S. companies and organizations. The DCS will create and make available an on-line performance rating form for use by our U.S. Citizens to evaluate their personal experience with a federal bureaucrat. There will be a separate form used by corporations and organizations. The completed forms are to be emailed or mailed back to the DCS and will by penalty of law, keep the name of the individual citizen, company or organization confidential. The DCS will analyze and combine the evaluations into one report every six months. This portion of the report will reflect our citizens' experiences with the federal bureaucrat. The on-line evaluations forms will cover such areas as:

- Did they clearly define/explain the subject matter?
- Did they provide all backup material?
- Were they courteous and well mannered?
- Were they overbearing or discourteous?
- Did they offer workable solutions?
- Did they threaten a fine or legal action?
- Did they solve the issue to your satisfaction?
- Was the matter brought up for arbitration?
- On a scale of 1 to 10 with 1 being lowest and 10 being highest, how would you rate your personal experience?
- What suggestions did you offer to resolve the issues?

These two separate evaluations (part one and part two) will be blended into one report every six months and this work will be performed by DCS.

• **Their second responsibility** will be to determine all salary budgets for each of these Departments and their Agencies. They will have sole responsibility for all salary budgets. Some departmental salary budgets and some agency budgets will decline, others will be flat and still others will increase depending upon the performance evaluations as published in the previous year. The DCS will also be the sole creator of all incentive bonus programs for each department. Each of these departmental budgets will be approved through a voting process involving all Civilian Agents and will require a simple majority vote. This budget will also reflect the prior year's performance appraisals.

The DCS salary and incentive budget recommendations will be forwarded to the House of Representatives as part of the Fiscal Budgeting Process.

How the DCS is to be Manned

The DCS will be manned via a voting process by the various state legislatures. Each state legislature will select two civilian representatives to a three year term as Civilian Agents of the DCS. These agents cannot be elected officials past or present; they cannot be lobbyists or campaign contributors and they cannot be friends or family of state politicians or government workers or work with any political party or special interest group. They are to be private citizens with at least two years of college education and at least ten years of practical work experience in the private market. The salary and expenses for these individuals will be paid by the appropriate state. All staffing personnel will be hired by each state and they will also be employees of the individual state. All expenses associated with the DCS will be paid by each state. The staff will report and work for the citizen agents and the agents will report to their own state legislatures. They will not report to the state governor or the governor's office. In that way, it is hoped they will remain as close to the U.S. Citizen as practically possible.

The DCS office building will be located in Washington D.C. and will be housed in one of the unoccupied office buildings as mentioned in Chapter 12.

The Citizen Agents will be allowed to serve only one term. Rather than have all terms end at one time, it is suggested that one third of the terms expire every year, in that way freshman agents make up roughly one third of the whole. Yes, that will mean that some of the initial agents will serve only one year or two year terms but I should think that would be preferable to having all terms ending at the same time.

The Purpose of the DCS

The purpose of the DCS is to keep our government bureaucrats mindful of the fact that they work for and ultimately report to the U.S. Citizen. Its purpose follows the same reasoning that mandated that our military reports to a civilian. Our military has been held in check, our federal bureaucrats have not. **As we are finding out, that has been a mistake, especially when we have an activist President who has hijacked his department's bureaucrats and turned them into his party's elite political strong arms.** They are encouraged by Obama to operate in lieu of our elected legislature. They are only restrained when they are being asked to investigate major misdeeds of the administration. They are enforcing laws following political guidelines, not legal statutes.

While you may agree with the politics of President Obama, what will you have to say when another President takes an opposite political approach? What will be in place to stop him/her from taking an even stronger approach in the opposite direction? Will you be complaining then? Impeachment is not the answer nor is shutting down the government.

But we cannot suffer these abuses without implementing a long lasting solution; we cannot allow any President to rule by political fiat; we cannot allow any President to ignore a wide spectrum of statues because they are not aligned with his political party. We cannot allow a President to ignore a co-equal branch of our government and take the law into his/her own hands. A free society will not long endure if bureaucrats are allowed to make their own rule of law and enforce statutes of their liking while giving statute immunity to huge swaths of law breakers. We need to bring these bureaucrats to heal in a Constitutional manner and place the power where it belongs, with the U.S. Citizen and the States.

Excessive regulation is the fourth major cause of our Wealth Gap.

These regulations are preventing entrepreneurs from forming new companies and they are preventing existing companies from hiring any new employees.

I realize that this is a very bold program. I realize that this will require a lot of debate but in the end it is an idea that will enhance the lives of our U.S. Citizens and bring our oversized and overbearing government under the control of We the People. The states will like it as well!

CHAPTER 15

Muscle, Juice, Punch, Power
We Have It, They Don't

Can you hear it? It is screaming at you! You are just not
listening hard enough! It's the silence itself. It is telling you
something important but are you listening? Let me be your
interpreter. Five years ago, the airwaves were full of panic and
concern. No, I am not writing about the stock market or the
banks' failures. It's the oil market! We were running out of
oil, the world was running out of oil; we were tapping out
known reserves and we were not finding enough new oil to
keep up with the pace of demand. And so began the drumbeat
of cries to do more with less; we needed to lower our fuel
demand: less driving, higher mileage vehicles, alternative
energy vehicles. We must downsize, we must decrease our
environmental footprint, and we must blah, blah, blah... It was
all a lot of rubbish. It was a manmade event and was
orchestrated by a few well placed special interests.

What was really happening was the oil companies wanted
to raise the price of oil and refined fuel. The environmentalists
wanted to raise the price of energy to make alternative energy
more viable. Once prices were up, there was plenty of oil and
no one was telling you that we are out of oil. But think about
it, are there more people on the planet today than five years
ago? Do you think that there are more cars and more semi-

trucks and more airplanes? All of this increased demand on a global level and yet there is now so much oil that prices are falling and the oil companies are turning off the oil pumps. Do you see how they are playing us as fools? We need to quit being fools!

The truth is that oil companies only pump enough oil to meet demand and their pricing needs. It is not a matter of running out of oil, just managing availability to support the prices they want to receive.

Now, there is a fly in their soup. The fly is hydraulic fracturing. As often happens, USA ingenuity has overcome the obstacles that prevented a profitable means to extract oil from the sands and shale that hold oil. So, voilà! The USA is on its way to becoming a self-sufficient oil producer. There is now no way of hiding the fact that we are and always have been an energy independent nation. The problem now is that the big oil interests want to export USA crude oil to the world. Here comes another big special interest push and secret meetings with politicians to persuade them to approve the export of crude oil. At the present time it is not allowed by law and it should never be allowed. This is one of our advantages and it needs to remain our exclusive advantage.

Let's not forget coal and natural gas; two additional major sources of energy which are abundant in our country. We are already exporting coal and we are working on exporting our natural gas in a frozen and compacted state

which will increase the amount of gas that can be shipped by
tankers.

Enter the Problem

As I have already stated, now that our jobs have migrated
to China and other third world countries, these same countries
are now buying the natural resources that are needed to fuel
their growing economies. What better place than the USA to
supply their needs. The U.S. no longer has a need for all their
natural wealth and besides the USA has to export something
don't we? The refined petroleum products that they are
currently buying from us today are not sufficient. They need
the raw resources. So the question is; will we sell out our
natural resources beneath our feet? Are we just another
Australia? Australia's only major exports are their natural
resources. Is that all we have to offer? And who came up with
global pricing? Why is the U.S. Citizen paying the same for
U.S. extracted natural resources as anyone worldwide? Are
there no tax advantages given to these companies by the U.S.
Citizen? Do you think that lower homeland energy prices
would be a competitive advantage for what remains of our
manufacturing? Does China's policy favor their homeland or
do they charge their citizens and manufacturers a global price?
One of their key resources is a huge labor pool. Do they make

sure that labor charges a salary based on a global average or do they keep labor wages extremely low to advantage their country? What about Germany? They, like Japan, need to import most of their energy needs. Should they be on a level plane with us? We have the energy, we have the natural resources and they don't. Why are we not using this to our exclusive advantage?

We should be offering our domestic market lower energy costs that will provide an advantage to our local manufacturers and will reduce the bite that high energy costs are taking out of our citizens' pocketbooks. As I stated in my Comments, we need to leverage our advantages to benefit the U.S. Citizen and the U.S. Economy.

The Conservative Solution
Plank Nine
Advantage USA

In 1804 Lewis and Clark began the Corps of Discovery Expedition. It was one of the most pivotal expeditions ever undertaken by our government. They explored and reported on their findings regarding our land purchase from France; something called the Louisiana Purchase.

I propose that we now initiate an Energy Corps of Discovery Expedition. A team consisting of geologists, oceanologists and oil, gas and coal experts is to be assembled and tasked with mapping and measuring all of our country's natural energy resources. Their work will be our starting place.

Second, I propose that we put together another team of scientists and accountants that will produce a report on the value of ethanol. The report will analyze and rate the most dollar effective raw material that can be used per unit of energy produced, offset by the energy required to produce and transport the ethanol. The report will also analyze the greenhouse gases produced by the manufacturing of these products as well as those gasses produced by the burning of these various ethanol products. The results will be compared to every other gasoline formula. Remember, that I stated a Conservative will never require the U.S. Citizen to pay for things that are not in their best interest.

140

Third, we need a definitive report on clean coal processes versus natural gas when used to generate electricity. Which provides a kilowatt of energy at the lowest cost? Analyze the greenhouse gases produced by each process and scale the results. I would ask Ohio State University to produce this report as they have done a lot of research work on extracting the energy in coal without burning it, but rather utilizing a chemical process. Does this have any commercial potential or not? Is this something that the country should invest in to secure a source of low cost energy without carbon being released? If so, then this would have a positive and significant impact on all our U.S. Citizens.

Fourth, we need a similar report on natural gas for use in transportation.

After these reports are completed, a comprehensive energy plan will be written that advantages our economy and our U.S. Citizens. One that will provide critical support toward the jobs program that I recommended in Chapter 9. We have the natural resources and the ingenuity to be able to provide ample, cheap and clean energy. All we have lacked is the political will to make it happen.

Now that prices are down, Congress is talking about raising the gas tax now that gas prices are low. I suggest they first produce a report detailing where all the current gas taxes have been spent for the last twenty years. I am quite sure that these tax dollars are not going to general road repair but let's see what they find; that is, if and when they produce such a

141

report. We do not need more tax dollars going to pet projects and not general road repair. In the minds of our politicians in Washington D.C. enough is never enough when it comes to tax collections.

Federal taxes are: 18.4 cents per gallon of gasoline and 24.4 cents per gallon of diesel fuel. In 2013 there were about 134.51 billion gallons of gasoline consumed and about 36.5 billion gallons of diesel fuel. The combined total federal taxes collected in 2013 exceeded $33.68B. Now keep in mind that the federal government only contributes 25% to highway repair and new construction and the states contribute the other 75%, so 33.68B really represents a potential $134.7B annual budget to repair roads. That is a significant annual budget and one that exceeds our current needs. The problem is that all of the gas and fuel tax revenue is not spent on road and bridge repair.

The bottom line, we are an energy independent country; we just need to announce it and we need to maintain it. It will make a significant and positive difference in our lives. It will also make a difference in our foreign policies and relationships when dealing with the various Middle East countries.

CHAPTER 16

Unreported Weapons of Mass Destruction
What Are They And What Needs To Be Done

Here I have cobbled together seven areas that have raised my red flag. None of these areas are being reported in the press and I am bringing them to your attention for the purposes of focusing on them and offering proposed solutions.

The Conservative Solutions
Plank Ten
Seven Deadly and Costly WMD's

<u>High-Frequency Trading</u>

Have you ever heard the name Sergey Aleynikov? No? Well you should know that he is a former software programmer that worked at Goldman Sachs. It seems that Sergey had a little more on his mind than just giving Goldman Sachs the product of his skills; he wanted to take the entire program he was working on for himself. Back in June, 2009 he downloaded and stole the source code for Goldman's high-frequency trading program. Goldman Sachs was immediately alarmed and they brought in the FBI who initiated a manhunt. It seems at the time, that Goldman Sachs was very concerned because this particular software could be used by terrorists to do untold harm to the U.S. stock markets. In short, he stole a Weapon of Mass Destruction.

The programming source code was a high-frequency trading program, also called flash trading by some. It seems that with this program, an individual could cause huge irregularities and possible crashes in all of our equity markets. To say the least, that was very alarming. Well, Sergey was arrested and sentenced to an 8 year prison term for stealing company trade secrets.

All of the news agencies reported on the story and following the prison sentence, the story ended. But as usual the press did a lousy job of identifying the real story. The real story was not about Sergey stealing trade secrets. <u>The real story is; what is Goldman Sachs doing with a Weapon of Mass Destruction</u>? If this software program can cause this kind of destruction, why is Goldman allowed to use it? If it can do this kind of destruction, what can it do on a smaller scale? Is Goldman manipulating our markets for their own gain? Do you wonder? I wonder.

What's worse, there are many other companies that are using similar software and performing the same functions.

And the Security and Exchange Commission has amplified their ability to move markets by allowing them to place their computers in the same room as the exchange computers. The purpose of that action is to further reduce the time it takes to trade stock by a few milliseconds. Imagine that? The SEC is an enabler to these flash traders. I wonder why the individual stock investor has left the market. Do you think that the Federal Reserve has teamed up with the owners of these software programs and manipulated our stock markets? Take a look at most of the stock prices of many companies. The prices are completely decoupled from the fundamental results of these companies. Many companies' sales results have been flat or falling but their stock prices are rising. Flat and decreasing sales are a sign that the economy is shrinking but by some miracle their stock prices are rising.

145

Regardless, these high-frequency trading programs need to be prohibited and their computers need to be removed from the secret location where our exchange computers are housed. It is one thing to use electronic trading; it is another to allow the use of flash trading programs that clearly advantage the wealthy and the well connected.

These programs are the fifth reason we are seeing the wealth gap back at historical highs.

We need an answer to this question, "What are these companies doing with WMD's?"

Inner City Neighborhoods and Gangs

The poor are not well connected. Their neighborhoods are not safe and little is being done to make them safe. Gunfire and police sirens are so common they are just considered background noise and are for the most part, ignored. We can no longer ignore the plight of these U.S. Citizens.

They are being terrorized on a daily basis and we are doing little to solve the problems. I propose that all violent gangs be reclassified as terrorists' organizations, for that is what they are, terrorists. I recommend that we confiscate their bank accounts and any other property they own as a group and/or individually. A policing action needs to be conducted to identify members of these gangs and then we should apply existing anti-terrorist statutes to remove these individuals from the neighborhoods in which they dwell. We have no excuse for inaction. The U.S. Citizens who live in these areas have every right to live in a peaceful and safe neighborhood. We can no longer allow these gangs to rule and ruin their lives. We can no longer allow the slaughtering of innocent women, men and children at the hands of these terrorists.

Artificial Intelligence and Robotics

It is coming at us like a freight train and we need to control its direction and speed. Advancements are rapidly coming in the areas of A.I. and Robotics and we as a nation need to formulate guideline policies before there is a problem. This is similar to the human cloning issues that were raised and dealt with several years ago. We must get in front of any potential problems that may emerge from our work and all international work in these area. A global understanding and agreement must also be reached that covers both the civilian as well as the commercial and military markets.

It is forecasted that within the next 10 to 20 years we will experience a commercial revolution in the use of robotics and A.I. These forecasts also state that many of our jobs that exist today will be replaced with robots. That is well indeed, if on the other hand we have other meaningful and significant work for our citizens to perform. If not, then we will be staring at a very significant social problem that may have the potential to become very messy. This area really needs to be thought through and handled correctly in advance. I suggest we do the thinking and planning and policy making now to make sure that we are protecting the best interests of our U.S. Citizens. And by the way, can you think of a way that a terrorist might want to place a bomb on an autonomous robot?

Pandemic

We are currently in the middle of handling the most recent Ebola outbreak and it seems that we were not as prepared as we once thought. This has been a wakeup call and we should pay heed and better prepare our responses. We have not adequately prepared our medical staffs in advance, not prepared our medical facilities in advance, not prepared our quarantine procedures in advance, our transportation systems were not prepared and we most certainly were not properly prepared to secure our borders in advance. I suggest that we think this through again and have the plan and the required equipment in place. Further, we must train all medical personnel on an ongoing basis starting now. And just

for arguments sake, do you think it would be easier to
quarantine all potential carriers before they enter the country
or do you think it is easier to track down all the people and
places they have been in contact with during their time in our
country?

Secondly, why are we allowing Yoshihiro Kawaoka of
the University of Wisconsin-Madison to modify a strain of
pandemic flu which allows it to ignore our body's immune
systems? In short, we will all die if this one escapes. Do you
think this could be weaponized? Is there anyone on this Earth
outside of a rogue nation or a terrorist organization who thinks
this is a smart idea? Maybe a pharmaceutical company may
like it but even I would doubt that one. There is no other word
to describe this except "insane". How many other scientists are
out there doing the same thing with different diseases? Without
a doubt this is a Weapon of Mass Destruction and should never
have been allowed. Our citizens need to be made aware that
this particular case has been handled and that these types of
research will not be allowed.

Finally, many if not most of our antibiotics are being
produced in China. How this ever passed the smell test is
beyond me but apparently it is happening. I recommend that
we review our sourcing regarding all medications and that we
bring back to this country all manufacturing of critical
medications. I wonder what other critical items we are
allowing Communist China to exclusively manufacture. I

think we should find out.

Individual Foreign Money Transfers

On an individual basis money transfers to other countries
are not alarming and are a necessary daily activity for many
who are here in our country. The real harm that is occurring is
when it is taking place on a mass scale. Billions of dollars are
leaving this country every year and are being used to build the
economies of other countries and not ours. As we all know,
the circulation of money within a country's borders improves
the economy and the lives of its citizens. I am concerned that
this transfer of wealth is having a significant and negative
impact on the daily lives of all U.S. Citizens. We need to keep
these Billions of dollars circulating within our country to build
our economy. In addition, there are so many small money
transfers that it is likely that drug money is being laundered
through these transfers. It is not my intention to stop these
transfers but rather, we need to make sure that they are
legitimate and that all taxes have been paid on the money
before the transfer is made.

I propose that individuals who wish to transfer money to
another country provide proof that taxes were paid on this

money. The simple procedure to be followed would entail the individual to complete a federal income tax form and receive proof of payment from the IRS in the form of a tamper-proof card. The card would declare that the card holder is allowed to transfer a certain amount of money limited to the total after tax amount declared on their previous year's tax filing. To receive the card, a checked box on the tax form needs to be marked and the IRS will send a card to the individual after the form is processed. A processing fee will also be imposed to cover the cost of the program. The U.S. Citizens should not pay for this program. If the amount earned is not subject to taxes, then the card will reflect the entire earned amount. The various money transfer companies will be tied into this card system and will only transfer individual funds for card holders and will limit total transfer amounts to the total detailed on the card. The transfer companies will also charge an incremental fee to cover their costs for this new program. It is that simple.

Self-Driving Vehicles

A self-driving vehicle sounds great! It would be convenient, hopefully safe and would allow passengers to spend their time more productively or for that matter, they could just take a nap.

151

The big problem is that every terrorist would pack these vehicles with explosives and have them driven into any crowded area in any city. I am sure they would view them as a gift from heaven. We on the other hand might have a few problems with this one. It is not too hard to imagine semi-trucks packed with explosives doing untold damage at numerous locations, all happening at the same time. We need to think this one through a little longer.

Google

Google is truly an innovative company that provides a great service to all computer users. I have no problem with their product or their service. My concern is that they are expanding into more and more areas like healthcare and these new services will allow them to know more and more about us on an individual basis. I do not think that any one company should have this much information about any of us, let alone all of us.

In addition, they are also focusing on offering services to children 12 years and under. This warrants a lot of concern on my part.

We should look into the scope of this company and think long and hard about individual privacy versus Google's extended reach into our lives. We should be looking closely at building a firewall between them and the U.S. Citizen.

Remember the work of Teddy Roosevelt and how he dealt with companies that controlled too much of any one area. The area of my concern is that Google knows too many intimate details about each U.S. Citizen.

We do not need a privately owned "Big Brother" watching our every move, let alone a governmental one acting in the same way. We need to reduce Google's everyday presence in our lives and limit the amount of information that they can retain at any one time.

CHAPTER 17
The Pecking Order
Our Current Position Is Not Acceptable

Dear Reader:

At this point in the book, it seems appropriate to clearly demonstrate to you how we are ranked by each political party and by most of their elected officials. As neither party has ever claimed to be on the side of the U.S. Citizen, I wish to provide you with where I believe we rank in importance within each political party. You may quibble with some of my rankings, but directionally, the U.S. Citizen is ignored and/or taken for granted. You may, if you wish, ask your representative or senator where they rank the U.S. Citizen versus their special interests and then ask what actions they have taken that best demonstrate their claim.

A Pecking Order is the method by which chickens sort out the dominance of each bird from highest to lowest rank. The more dominate bird pecks the lower one and in such a manner, they set a hierarchy of authority within their flock.

I think it is important to understand just where we stand within the present power structure in Washington D.C. Therefore, I have, through my own observations, determined the pecking order that each political party has established through their own actions. Here are my own rankings based on these observations. I think it is enlightening and informative to know where we stand within their political hierarchy. This I think is the real world order of Washington D.C. and it will give you a proper and realistic perspective of where you and I fit into their concept of the New World Order.

The Democrat Party Pecking Order

Highest to Lowest
• DemoParty Office Holders - National Level
• DemoParty Leaders - National Level
• DemoParty Office Holders - State and Local
• DemoParty Leaders - State and Local
• Big Banks and Hedge Fund Managers
• Trial Attorneys
• NAACP
• Big Business
• Environmentalists
• Civil Rights Organization Members
• Conservationists
• Women Rights Organizations
• AARP
• Planned Parenthood
• Unions
• Animal Rights Organizations
• Various Liberal and Progress Think Tanks

155

- Liberal Boogers
- Illegal Immigrants - the Future Power Base
- Government Bureaucrats - Federal
- Government Bureaucrats - State and Local
- Foreign Companies and Foreign Workers
- Dog Catchers
- Police Departments and Policemen
- U.S. Citizens - Last Again.

The Republican Party Pecking Order

Highest to Lowest
- Establishment Republican Office Holders - National Level
- Establishment Republican Party Leaders - National Level
- Establishment Republicans - State and Local Level
- Chamber of Commerce
- Various Business Organizations
- Big International Business
- Big Hedge Fund Managers
- Big Banks
- Defense Contractors
- Various Police Organizations
- Various Tax Reducing Organizations
- Various Religious Organizations

- Conservative Republican Office Holders - National Level
- Conservative Republicans - State and Local Level
- Conservative Think Tanks
- Conservative Boogers
- Foreign Companies and Foreign Workers
- Illegal Immigrants
- Dog Catchers
- U.S. Citizens – Still Last Again

The Conservative Pecking Order
Our Proper Place

Highest to Lowest
- The U.S. Citizen
- True Conservative Politicians
- Freedom and Liberty focused Organizations
- Conservative Think Tank Organizations
- Small Business Organizations
- Law and Order Organizations
- Libertarian Organizations
- Religious Organizations
- Policing Organizations
- Medical and Health Organizations
- Veteran Organizations

157

- Establishment Republicans
- Big Business
- Dog Catchers
- Self Serving Politicians
- Lobbyists
- Special Interest Groups

Now, which group do you want to belong to and which group will you support?

As a side note, if you are ever in Washington D.C., take a look at some of our Federal Congressional and Senatorial offices. Not the outer offices but the politician's actual office. You will notice that most of them have an ego wall of pictures; the ones taken with famous politicians or celebrities. These office holders are all about themselves. The offices that have a wall of pictures featuring their constituents are the offices that belong to the best of our representatives. These are the men and women who know that their life is about helping the people they represent. This little excursion will tell you everything you need to know!

CHAPTER 18

An Urgent 2015 Republican Response
Gardening Skills And Gardening Etiquette
The Case Of The Deferring Referee

Once upon a time, in a land not so far away, there were two gardens that supplied all the fruits and vegetables to the inhabitants of their land. As the population grew so did the size of these gardens. Each year the gardens were provided the required funding by the inhabitants so that they could continue to run their organizations. For many, many years these gardens worked side by side and were focused upon doing their best for the inhabitants of their land.

In the beginning, the wisest of the inhabitants created a law that set these two gardens apart. That law required each garden to focus on providing separate products for the satisfaction and nutrition of the citizens. One garden was given authority over all vegetables and the other was given authority over all fruits. As they each tended their gardens, they grew in strength and numbers, but because of their mammoth size they would argue over whose product was shipped first and whose garden received more water than the other, what pesticides they were allowed to use and so forth. At times the fighting got so bad that neither one of them would give in to the other. But the wise inhabitants had foreseen such a problem and they also wrote into the law an

159

equally important position of referee. The referee position was to keep peace between the two gardens and, as I stated, all went well for many, many years. Yes, there were times when the referees had to make a decision and when it was made, both gardens accepted their decision and they went on working side by side for the benefit of the population.

But there were other differences between these gardens that the wise ones wrote into their law. The fruit garden was run by one person who hired many workers to till the soil, tend to the plants and then harvest the product. The vegetable garden was run by the consent of two groups of people who operated as one person.

As time went by, the fruit garden would take on the personality of the one in charge. It was this person who would move his workers around and direct them to work on different things, the things he viewed as important. So, sometimes these workers would concentrate on improving the soil and sometimes they would concentrate on producing better fruit trees or better fertilizer. All of these actions were the product of one leader's direction, but at no time could this leader decide to grow vegetables. That was strictly forbidden and the referee position was there to make sure that it never happened.

The vegetable garden was a different matter. Because it required the agreement of so many different individuals, they did not always agree on what needed to be done. For instance, some thought they should concentrate on improving the water filtration system and others wanted to improve their shipping

160

methods and so on. Sometimes it seemed that nothing got done, but in the end they always produced great vegetables. It was the decision making process that always concerned the inhabitants, but they accepted the fact that getting a majority to agree and manage a garden could be messy and besides, the products of their labors were always fresh, safe, plentiful and healthy. But some in the population complained because they did not like certain vegetables produced by this garden. Broccoli and brussel sprouts were always criticized and many in the land did not want them to be grown; but some liked these two awful tasting vegetables, so they continued to be supplied. Regardless, the gardeners in the vegetable garden were always criticized for making their decisions so slowly and for making decisions that some in the population did not like. But the inhabitants agreed with most of their decisions and they understood the wisdom of allowing opposing views. When the inhabitants raised an objection to one of their decisions, they went to the referees for the final decision.

And so the gardens grew side by side and all was well, until one of the new leaders of the fruit garden decided that he should be able to grow vegetables as well as fruit. He started very slowly, growing only the two most popular vegetables. This alarmed many in the vegetable garden and they were calling on the leader of the fruit garden and telling him that he was not allowed to grow vegetables. But the leader said he was only growing two vegetables and that he was only trying to give the population more of what they wanted.

161

The vegetable gardeners went to the head referees to ask for a ruling but the referees deferred to the lower level refs. The head referees told the Veggiemen that they needed to begin their pleadings with the lowest ranking referee and then and only then proceed to the next higher referee. This is called 'deferring' and the head referees love it. The problem for the vegetable gardeners was that this process would take years and in the meantime the fruit gardeners were toiling in their patch. As can be expected they debated and discussed and debated and discussed and they finally came up with three other possible responses other than the lawsuit.

These are the three actions they may take against the fruit garden's encroachment:

1) Water flowed through their garden before it reached the fruit garden and they could cut off all the water to the fruit garden. They did this twice before but all that did was make the inhabitants very unhappy as their source of fruit was cut off. They blamed the vegetable gardeners not the fruit gardeners.

2) They could make the public aware of the situation and hope that they could produce a ground swell of sentiment against the fruit gardener in hopes that they would stop growing vegetables due to public pressure.

3) They could contest the nomination of any future fruit gardeners. This does not resolve the encroachment issue, but it would get the leader of the fruit garden's attention.

162

Alas, their responses produced no immediate termination of the fruit gardeners actions. The fruit gardeners continued to grow vegetables. The longer they were able to grow them, the more they wanted to grow all the vegetables and cut out the vegetable gardeners altogether. That soon became their goal; to eradicate the gardeners in the vegetable garden and take control of all fruits and vegetables. If they were able to gain control over both gardens, they would in effect be able to control the eating habits of all the inhabitants of the land. This it turns out is their ultimate goal.

What made all of this possible was the absence of the head referees. They were blind to the acuteness of the problem. Perhaps they were eating too much fruit? The vegetable gardeners needed to find a way to get the immediate attention of the head referees before the fruit gardener became an established source for vegetables.

Unfortunately, they did not have a clue how they could quickly resolve this conflict.

As you may have surmised, the vegetable garden is our Congress, the fruit garden is our Executive Branch and the head referees are our deferring Supreme Court.

An Unexpected Solution
The Case of Bold Versus Bold

How Republicans Can Compel
The Supreme Court into Action

The real problem is how to immediately get this case in front of the Supreme Court. Continued inaction on their part will only allow the Executive Branch more time to encroach upon Congressional powers. I have a way this can be done, but it may not suit everyone, as it will require bold action on the part of Congress. John Boehner talks boldly but his actions are very measured and timid. In fact, I believe that he and many of the Establishment Republicans are in favor of Obama's immigration actions as Boehner seems to be tied at the hip with big business. His views do not represent the U.S. Citizen. I hope I am wrong and we will know by March 2015.

But if Boehner is true to his word about opposing Obama's actions, then here is my suggestion:

I recommend that Congress produce a Constitutional crisis to match that of the Executive Branch. The idea is to force the Supreme Court to act quickly to avoid an even larger crisis when two branches of our government are overreaching. It is unfortunate that another crisis is required but our system of justice is ill prepared to quickly resolve such bold actions

164

by the Executive Branch. Added to the mix is the fact that Mr. Obama is our first black President and no one wants to impeach him and deal with the false accusations of being called a racist. It is his actions that are being challenged not the color of his skin. Regardless, his race protects him and it makes impeachment an unacceptable option.

There is only one acceptable response which will get this issue in front of the Supreme Court. We all remember the Gore v. Bush Florida case; it was quickly accepted and adjudicated by the Supreme Court. It was the urgency of the situation that forced the Supreme Court to immediately accept the case. This urgency is required once gain or the DemoParty White House will continue to subordinate Congressional powers. That means that the Congress must cause its own Constitutional crisis to match that of the Executive Branch but they must do so without causing any problems for our U.S. Citizens.

Currently it is the Executive Branch that has sole authority to make judicial, ambassadorial and Cabinet nominations. As we are learning about Obama's pick for the next Attorney General, I suggest that Congress ignore all his current and future nominations. Further, I recommend that Congress take on the sole authority to make these nominations and usurp the powers of the Executive Branch. (Referencing my analogy above, Congress needs to do a little gardening in the Executive Branch's garden.) I recommend that the new Republican Congress ignore the President's nominations and claim that he had chosen to ignore their choices and they are tired of waiting for him to get it right, so they are taking the nomination authority upon themselves. **The House should nominate all candidates for all vacancies within the Executive Branch and the Senate should approve them now that the filibuster rules have been changed.** Congress should totally ignore all nominees coming from the Executive Branch just like the Executive Branch is ignoring Congress in the areas of immigration and environmental issues. This will send the message to Mr. Obama that two can play his game. It will shock the DemoPress and make them sit up and take notice. As two of the major branches of government are not playing nice in the sandbox, the third branch will be required to resolve and actually make a decision on both issues. Should the Supreme Court continue to hide behind their robes, then Congress should have their approved nominees attempt to take their designated positions.

The action I am recommending does not harm the U.S. Citizen but it will send a clear message to the Executive Branch as well as to the Supreme Court that if one branch can overreach, so can another. The Supreme Court needs to get off the sideline and do its job!

I do not see a downside to this action. The Constitutional scholars will grin and show a great deal of interest in how the Supreme Court resolves these issues. Our founding fathers showed great wisdom in establishing three co-equal branches of government to limit any one from dominating the other. It is time for the Supreme Court to recognize overreaching when they see it and to know it is time for them to act like an equal branch and put an end to it.

The Republican Congress needs to fight boldness with boldness.

Get hardnosed and stand up against the DemoParty!

CHAPTER 19

Into The Starting Gate
Primaries And The General Election

I believe that these ten planks making up a Conservative Platform are enough to separate a Conservative candidate from any other Republican primary candidate. In addition, they are broad based in appeal and they clearly define the difference between a Conservative and any progressive DemoParty candidate.

These proposals define Conservative principles and values in the correct way. Until now, the DemoParty has done its best to define Conservatives as mean and cold hearted people who only care about the rich and hate all women and old people. These proposals define the Conservative Movement as the champion of our middle class and position them squarely behind the U.S. Citizen. They draw a clear and positive distinction between Conservatives and the Establishment Republicans. They hone more clearly the qualities and values that were championed by President Reagan. These proposals offer a platform from which a Conservative candidate can win the White House in 2016.

These proposals give the Tea Party supporters a broader based agenda that they can support, and it is my thought that they will show strong support for them.

I acknowledge that there are many other issues that I did not touch upon but covering every possible domestic and foreign policy issue was not the purpose of this book.

I firmly believe that these proposed planks will provide a Conservative candidate a significant advantage in the primary and in the general election debates. Conversely, they will hinder the candidate's ability to raise money from many special interest groups, but I think that is resolvable.

If by some measure of fortune, these proposals allow a Conservative to stand shoulder to shoulder with the other primary candidates upon the dais, then I think he/she will have one of the strongest closing arguments ever heard during any previous debate.

It is impossible to predict what questions will be asked during any of the debates, but these proposed closing remarks will result in winning over the voter in both the primary and general election debates.

Closing Statement in the Republican Primary Debates and the General Election Debates

For the first time in our history, your vote will determine if you have a government of the people or a government of the special interests. Your vote will determine if our great middle class will expand and grow or continue to shrink. Your vote

169

will determine if you have a government that unceasingly supports our U.S. Citizens or the citizens of the world. Your vote will determine if we pass on to our children a country on the verge of bankruptcy or a more solvent and prosperous country. Your vote will affect the lives of many, many future generations of U.S. Citizens.

If you want a government that lies to you, then vote for my opponent(s).

If you want a government that makes secret backroom deals with money men and lobbyists, then vote for my opponent(s).

If you want a government that places itself between you and everything in your life and then taxes you and micro manages your life, then vote for my opponent(s).

If you want a government that moves your job overseas, then vote for my opponent(s).

If you want a government within the government that makes its own laws and is not accountable to you, then vote for my opponent(s).

If you want a government that provides lifetime jobs to nameless bureaucrats whom enact laws that micro manage your life, then vote for my opponent(s).

If you want a government that financially rewards these lifetime bureaucrats for interfering in your life, then vote for my opponent(s).

If you want a big government that spends your tax dollars with no constraints, then vote for my opponent(s).

If you want a government that invades your privacy and actively spies upon you, then vote for my opponent(s).

If you want a government that supports and continues to build the wealth gap between rich and poor, then vote for my opponent(s).

If you want a government that pushes the middle class into poverty, then vote for my opponent(s).

If you want a government that allows the Federal Reserve to keep secret its actions which pad the pockets of the wealthy and kill job growth, then vote for my opponent(s).

If you want a government that favors special interest groups over the U.S. Citizen, then vote for my opponent(s).

If you want a government that is more concerned about foreign unemployment numbers rather than our country's unemployment, then vote for my opponent(s).

If you want a government that allows China to buy our natural resources out from under our feet, then vote for my opponent(s).

If you want a government that allows a communist government to buy key U.S. Corporations, then vote for my opponent(s).

If you want to see China and Russia grow their military and strengthen their alliance while we are shrinking our military, then vote for my opponent(s).

If you want lousy health insurance with higher deductibles and fewer doctors participating, then vote for my opponent(s). (To be used in the general election debate.)

But...

If you want a government that elevates the U.S. Citizen above all others, then I ask for your vote.

If you want a government that makes it illegal for government officials to lie to you, then I ask for your vote.

If you want a government that passes a law that places you, the U.S. Citizen, between the politician and special interest groups, then I ask for your vote.

If you want a government that offers a real jobs program, then I ask for your vote.

If you want a government that will actively shrink the wealth gap, then I ask for your vote.

If you want a government that encourages companies to invest in the USA in order to rebuild our country, then I ask for your vote.

If you want a government that makes the Federal Reserve's actions more transparent, then I ask for your vote.

If you want a government that values your right to privacy and watches those who threaten your safety, then I ask for your vote.

If you want a government that constrains it's spending and builds its budget from the ground up, then I ask for your vote.

If you want a government that pays government employees based on how well they serve you, the U.S. Citizen, then I ask for your vote.

If you want a government that will not micro manage your life, then I ask for your vote.

If you want better healthcare with more doctors, more nurses, more lab technicians staffing more convenient locations, then I ask for your vote.

If you want to restore the balance of power between the Executive Branch and Congress, then I ask for your vote.

I will do my utmost to improve your lives and the lives of your family members. I promise you that I will always maintain my focus on our U.S. Citizens and I will always cover your "6".

Thank you for listening and God Bless you and God Bless the USA!

Chapter 20

Summary

Washington D.C. is broken. The federal government only works for the special interest groups, large campaign donors and big business. They no longer work for the U.S. Citizen.

This book is about ideas that are focused on improving our lives, the lives of the U.S. Citizen. It is a book intended to create a meaningful discussion about 'We the People' and what kind of government we want and more importantly what kind of government we deserve. We must find a candidate who endorses these real solutions. Someone who will be our genuine representative, someone we can trust to do what is best for us, who will be honest with us and will listen to us. It is time to vote for someone who will have a positive impact upon our lives and the lives of future generations.

It is time to recognize our present politicians for what they are: self serving, manipulative, money hungry, power hungry individuals who only care about us during their election campaigns and then do the bidding of their biggest donors and special interest groups. They operate as if we are the problem. We are not the problem. They need to be reminded that they work for us. Their work needs to be focused on improving our lives, not improving the lives of the wealthy and the well connected or the foreign citizens.

Today's politician and their special interest organizations will tell you that this platform will never see the light of day; that it will never be enacted. I am here to tell you that it is not up to them, it is solely up to you. It is and always has been up to you and you alone.

We can have a real choice when we vote in 2016. We must stop voting for the lesser of two evils. We must start voting for someone who wants what is best for us; the U.S. Citizen.

If you believe that we can build a better economic environment, a better healthcare system, an honest government that has your best interests at the core of all their actions, and you are willing to vote for it, then it will happen. **The real question is: do you believe in yourself?**

www.ingramcontent.com/pod-product-compliance
Lightning Source LLC
Chambersburg PA
CBHW070649290526
45790CB00001B/235